SCOTT JOPLIN

SCOTT
A LIFE IN RAGTIME
JOPLIN

BY STEVEN OTFINOSKI

AN IMPACT BIOGRAPHY

FRANKLIN WATTS
A Division of Grolier Publishing
New York ~ London ~ Hong Kong ~ Sydney
Danbury, Connecticut

Cover illustration copyright ©: John DeGrace
Photographs copyright ©: Archive Photos: pp. 10 (Frank Driggs), 89
(Hackett); The Bettmann Archive: pp. 27, 30, 34, 36, 52, 62, 68,
73, 103; Culver Pictures: pp. 38, 74; UPI/Bettmann: pp. 56, 113;
Jim Caldwell/Houston Grand Opera Archives: pp. 81, 84, 92; New York
Public Library, Special Collections: p. 97; Photofest: p. 118.

Library of Congress Cataloging-in-Publication Data

Otfinoski, Steven.
Scott Joplin: a life in ragtime/by Steven Otfinoski.
p.   cm. — (An impact biography)
Includes bibliographical references (p.   ) and index.
Summary: The story of America's most famous composer of ragtime music.
ISBN 0–531–11244–6
1. Joplin, Scott, 1868–1917—Juvenile literature.
2. Composers—United states—Biography—Juvenile literature. [1. Joplin,
Scott, 1868–1917. 2. Composers. 3. Afro-Americans—Biography.]
ML3930.J66084 1995
780'.92—dc20
[B]   95–8526   CIP AC MN

CONTENTS

To Beverly, who makes her own beautiful music

MAPLE LEAF
MADNESS

*Oh go 'way man, I can hypnotize dis nation,
I can shake de earth's foundation wid de Maple
Leaf Rag!
Oh go way man, just hold yo' breath a minit,
For there's not a stunt that's in it, wid de Maple
Leaf Rag!*[1]

—*"Maple Leaf Rag Song" (1904)
lyrics by Sydney Brown*

Nobody seems to know how the Maple Leaf Club got its name. It might have been its founders' fondness for the maple leaf's distinctive shape (the maple leaf would later become the national emblem of Canada). One thing, however, is certain. From the day in 1898 when the Williams brothers—two black entrepreneurs— opened their business, the Maple Leaf Club, it was the most impressive pleasure palace in Sedalia, Missouri.

Located over a seed store, the club boasted a Victorian bar made of carved walnut, comfortable tavern chairs, pool and gaming tables, and decorative gas chandeliers.

Scott Joplin

A large room served as a gathering place for political and social groups. This same room served as a rehearsal hall for Sedalia's most prestigious musical ensemble—the all-black Queen City Concert Band.

But the biggest draw at the Maple Leaf Club in its first prosperous years was a thirty-one-year-old itinerant black musician and composer who played piano in the back-room with a dexterity and grace that was the talk of Sedalia. His name was Scott Joplin, but to the regulars, he was known simply as "The Entertainer."

Joplin hailed from Texarkana, Texas, and had settled in town about the time the Maple Leaf Club had opened.

One fateful summer's night in 1899, a refined fifty-eight-year-old man with a trimmed beard, thick mustache, and clear blue eyes walked into the Maple Leaf Club and ordered a drink. His name was John Stark and he owned a small music store in town. Stark was intrigued by the infectious piano music coming from the backroom and decided to take a closer look.

Scott Joplin was hardly the sporting district's typical piano player. He dressed conservatively, had a polite, almost shy, demeanor, and played his own compositions with a seriousness that was more becoming a concert hall than a saloon.

John Stillwell Stark was a businessman with taste who knew good music when he heard it. Born in Shelby County, Kentucky, on April 11, 1841, Stark grew up on a farm in Gosport, Indiana. He was twenty-one when the Civil War broke out and served as a bugler in the First Regiment of the Indiana Heavy Artillery Volunteers. While stationed in New Orleans, he met and married his wife Sarah Ann Casey.

After the war, Stark moved to Missouri and settled in the town of Cameron. Here he entered his first successful business venture—making ice cream and selling it from the back of a Conestoga wagon. Always interested in music, he soon began selling pianos and organs for the Jesse French firm.

In 1883 he moved to Sedalia, where he opened a music store two years later, selling everything from instruments to sheet music. John Stark and Son prospered despite competition from two other music stores in town. In 1895 Stark bought out one of his competitors, who owned the copyrights to seven pieces of sheet music. In this inauspicious way, Stark became a music publisher. His first acquisitions were hardly remarkable—a handful of sentimental ballads typical of the period. And then he heard Scott Joplin play in the backroom of the Maple Leaf Club.

Stark introduced himself to Joplin and asked him to stop by his office, in a redbrick building at 516 Ohio Street the next morning. He wanted Joplin to play his compositions again for him and his son and partner, Will.

What took place that following morning in the offices of Stark and Son is clouded in legend. The most popular account is given by Stark's daughter-in-law, who was present. According to her, Joplin arrived punctually with his sheet music and a small black boy. After the introductions, he sat down confidently at the Jesse French upright piano and played two of his compositions. The first, "Sunflower Slow Drag," he had written with his friend and former pupil Scott Hayden. But the second, "Maple Leaf Rag," was all Joplin. The catchy ragtime tune was Joplin's favorite of his compositions and he played it nightly at the club, in whose honor it was named. Although two publishers had turned it down, the piece had become extremely popular in Sedalia and had been proudly hailed by patrons as the club's anthem.

Stark liked the music. It was bouncy and joyful but had a classical restraint and complexity that took the publisher by surprise. It was that same complexity, however, that also caused him concern. Would the music-buying public, used to simple melodies and quaint ditties, be able to master this difficult new music, in which the left hand was kept as busy as the right?

Joplin may well have been aware of the publisher's reservations and may have brought the boy along as "insurance." While Joplin played, the boy danced to the toe-tapping music. The dance he did was probably that lively new Negro strut that was just beginning to catch on with white folks—the cakewalk. Stark was charmed by the boy, and with a little persuasion from his son—who loved ragtime and was himself a composer—the publisher was sold. Stark bought Joplin's "Maple Leaf Rag" for an advance and the promise of a one-cent royalty paid on every copy of the sheet music sold.

This may not sound extraordinary today, but at the time it was nothing less than revolutionary. No composer received regular royalties from publishers for his compositions. Even the great Stephen Foster, the composer of some of America's most beloved songs, was paid an outright fee for most of his compositions—and died in abject poverty. Stark was offering Joplin an opportunity to make money along with him if "Maple Leaf Rag" were a success. The fact that Stark was white and Joplin black made this arrangement even more incredible for its time.

The contractual agreement between the two men also allowed Stark to publish Joplin's further compositions for the next five years, although not exclusively. In fact, their relationship would last for nine remarkable years and become one of the most extraordinary in American musical history.

In late September 1899, the first copies of the "Maple Leaf Rag" arrived at Stark's store from a St. Louis printer. The cover of the sheet music pictured two black couples dressed to the nines, heading out for a night on the town, inevitably to a cakewalk dance. The cover drew upon an advertisement of the American Tobacco Company that featured the cakewalk. Initial sales were slow but steady. Stark and Son, like many small music publishers in the American heartland, was a "mom and pop" operation that basically served a local clientele.

By the end of a year, Stark had sold only 400 copies of Joplin's rag, earning the composer the meager sum of four dollars in royalties. But by the fall of 1900, the infectious rhythms of "Maple Leaf Rag" had caught the ear of the buyer at one of the country's largest chain stores— F. W. Woolworth. The Woolworth store patrons were soon clamoring for Joplin's rag, and thousands of orders flowed into Stark's small Sedalia offices.

Over the next six months 75,000 copies of "Maple Leaf Rag" were sold. The entire Stark family worked day and night to print, package and mail out the sheet music. The publisher suspended publication of all his other music to keep up with the demand. Stark used his profits in late 1900 to move to larger quarters in St. Louis, 130 miles away, where he set up a printing plant on Laclede Avenue.

The "Maple Leaf Rag" had become a musical phenomenon.

Although a few rags had been published before it, none of them had struck a chord with the American public like Joplin's jaunty composition. Dozens of versions of the rag were turned out for every kind of musical instrument and ensemble and in every conceivable style. It remained most popular, of course, on the piano. For those amateur musicians who couldn't master its difficult style, there was available for purchase a newfangled machine called a player piano that could play the music for them. All the person had to do was pump the piano's pedals with his or her feet and out would flow the strains of Joplin's music.

The "Maple Leaf Rag" started a ragtime craze that swept the country. Publishers, anxious to cash in on its popularity, reissued any sheet music they had in their stockroom, merely adding the word "ragtime" to the cover to catch the music lover's eye. The unsuspecting buyer might arrive home to find his new ragtime piece was a sentimental ballad bereft of any noticeable syncopation or rhythm.

As for Scott Joplin, he had become one of the best-known composers in America. People came from all over the Midwest to the Maple Leaf Club to see him perform his famous rag. When Joplin traveled to other cities and towns to perform, local clubs were renamed the "Maple Leaf Club" in his honor. By 1902, the "Maple Leaf Rag" had become the first piece of instrumental sheet music to sell more than a million copies. Ragtime, the first truly American music, reigned supreme—and Scott Joplin was its king.

THE BOY WONDER
OF TEXARKANA

He just got his own music out of the air.[1]

—old neighbor of Scott Joplin

The story of how John Stark came to publish the "Maple Leaf Rag" is told in at least three versions, one which is undoubtedly true. Unfortunately, we do not have even one version to turn to concerning many of the other events in Joplin's life.

Writing a full biography of Scott Joplin presents many challenges to the writer. There are many years in his life that we know little or nothing about. Even those periods of his life that are better documented than most are often sketchy at best. Why is there so little documentation on the life of a man who today is considered to be one of America's most important composers? There are several reasons.

Scott Joplin, although a prolific composer, wrote little about himself or his work. There is no cache of letters, no journals, diaries, articles or books. His only extended piece of writing that survives is a brief instructional manual for ragtime musicians. What we know about him must be gathered from old newspaper clippings and reminiscences of his contemporaries–musicians and composers who were his students and colleagues. Even these accounts must be taken with some skepticism, for many of these people were talking and writing in the 1950s and 1960s about a man they had known nearly a half century earlier.

Second, the music Joplin wrote was not considered art but commercial fodder, as disposable as yesterday's newspaper. It was beneath the consideration of the respectable musical establishment of his day and was not deemed worthy of review and analysis in musical journals. The few articles about Joplin and his music primarily appeared in the commercial press.

Finally, and most important of all, Scott Joplin was black. Black people in the United States in the nineteenth and early twentieth centuries were more or less invisible. They were not seen as individuals worthy of study by white society, even if they had become famous, as Joplin had in 1899 with the "Maple Leaf Rag." Black Americans existed in their own separate society. Although the music Joplin and his contemporaries created and played crossed racial lines, they themselves were cut off from white society and would remain so—well into the twentieth century.

For these reasons, the life of Scott Joplin is a far less finished piece of work today than any one of his rags. There are still many questions about the man and his life that remain unanswered and may never be answered. There are other facts about his life that have been interpreted differently by various writers and historians. Yet we know enough about him–his triumphs and his tragedies–to gain an understanding of who he was, what he achieved, and how, through courage, talent, and persistence, he helped change the musical face of America.

Scott Joplin was born in Bowie County, Texas, on November 24, 1868—almost exactly three years after the adoption of the Thirteenth Amendment to the U.S. Constitution, which officially ended slavery in the United

States. This amendment was the final outcome of the Civil War, which ended in April 1865 with the surrender of the main Southern army.

Among the some four million freed slaves in America was Scott's father, Giles Joplin, who worked picking cotton on a plantation in the Carolinas. Actually, Giles had been freed shortly before the Civil War by his master, who was perhaps more enlightened than others of his class. After the first flush of freedom had faded, Giles, like most ex-slaves, came to the grim realization that freedom did not guarantee a better life. The vast majority of freed slaves were illiterate and nearly penniless, having no skills other than the manual labor they had done all their lives.

The United States government tried to help, establishing the Freedmen's Bureau in 1865 to provide food, care for the ill, schools at which blacks could be educated, and a resettlement program to start them in new lives. But the problems were too immense to be easily solved. Most Southern blacks remained poor and became the targets of the anger and prejudice of defeated white Southerners.

In 1866, the same year that the Civil Rights Act was passed, guaranteeing the citizenship of black Americans, the Ku Klux Klan was organized. This secret society was made up of white Southerners who, under white hoods and the darkness of night, terrorized and murdered thousands of Southern blacks. Congress, led by the Radical Republicans of the North, did what they could to help, but by the early 1870s the nation was tired of the black issue and was ready to end the program of rebuilding a new South, known as Reconstruction.

By 1877, the last federal troops stationed in the South to safeguard black rights were withdrawn and southern white Democrats regained control of their state governments. New laws hindered blacks from voting or holding office and segregated them from whites in public places and institutions. These so-called Jim Crow laws were established to keep blacks in their "place."

To escape the racism of the South and start life anew, many ex-slaves headed west with their families. Texas was as far west as many got, including Giles Joplin. Northeast Texas, although Southern, was still an untamed frontier and offered a chance for black Americans to build new lives. There Giles met and married a freeborn black woman from Kentucky, Florence Givens, who was the caretaker of a local black church.

At first, Giles Joplin found life in Texas just as difficult as it had been back home in South Carolina. He and his bride made their living as sharecroppers, picking crops and getting paid miserably by white farmers for their back-breaking labor. But the railroad was headed through Texas, and Giles had hopes of getting a job laying track.

The Joplins settled in a region that straddled the northeast corner of Texas and southwestern Arkansas, to be named Texarkana by 1873. From its conception, Texarkana was one of the most unusual municipalities in the United States. The name was supposedly formed by a railroad surveyor from the letters of the three nearest states —Texas, Arkansas and Louisiana. Texarkana was located in two of these three states. The Texas side of town was mostly white and prosperous. The Arkansas side was predominately black and poor. This racial demarcation exists there to this day.

The Joplins—Scott, his five siblings, and their parents—lived on the Texas side of town in relative security. Giles worked laying track for the Iron Mountain and Southern Railroad, while Florence cleaned homes and ironed clothes for the white folks in town.

In the evening when work was done, there was no television, radio, or movies to amuse the family, so they learned to entertain themselves. The most popular form of family entertainment in the decades after the Civil War was music, most often played on a piano in the parlor. American historian James Parton wrote in 1867 that the piano was only less important to the American home than the kitchen stove. There were 25,000 American-made pianos sold each year in the country and nearly every middle-class home had one.

The Joplins were too poor to buy a piano, but music rang out nightly in their humble home. Giles was an accomplished violinist and in his slave days had been part of a plantation band that performed for white parties. Florence played the five-string banjo and had a lovely singing voice. Ossie, the eldest, and his sister Myrtle both sang. Robert and Willie, the two youngest brothers, learned the violin from their father. But the most musically gifted of the Joplins was Scott. Before he was seven he had taught himself the guitar and the bugle and played both skillfully.

That same year Scott discovered a piano in a neighbor's house and began fiddling on the keys. Without a lesson, he was soon playing like a professional. When his mother took him with her on her cleaning jobs in the homes of white people he often found a piano in the parlor. With the mistress of the house's permission, Scott would practice on the piano while his mother did her chores. He was soon improvising his own music based on the hymns and spirituals he heard in church, adding rhythms and harmonies derived from the black folk music his mother had taught him.

Florence Joplin was proud of her son's musical talent and scrimped and saved for a secondhand upright piano so he could play at home. Giles was just as proud of Scott's abilities, at first. But as the growing boy spent more and more time playing the piano, his father began to worry. He did not believe his son could make a living as a musician and wanted him to go to work for the railroad like himself.

His mother had a stronger faith in Scott's talent, and husband and wife argued over their son's future constantly. It eventually was one factor that led to Giles leaving home. Although he would remain in Texarkana and see his family regularly, Giles Joplin would never live with his wife again. Another son, Monroe, the only nonmusical member of the family, got a job as a cook and left home soon after his father. Florence moved with her five remaining children to the Arkansas side of town, where she could find a house with a cheaper rent.

Life became harder for the family, but Scott's mother would not deny her son his chance at a musical career. When he was thirteen, she started him on piano lessons. His first teacher was Mag Washington, a woman who taught in a black school Scott attended. His most influential teacher, however, was an extraordinary man named J. C. Johnson. Some biographers claim Johnson was a German; others, that he was black or mulatto. Whatever his background, Johnson was an excellent music teacher who immediately recognized the rare talent of his young pupil—and gave him piano lessons for free. The "Professor," as he was called, introduced Scott to the world of classical music—especially the piano music of Bach, Mozart, and Beethoven. He taught Scott about such classical forms as sonatas, symphonies, and fugues. He also introduced the young musician to opera, that fascinating melding of drama and music, which would have a profound effect on Scott in later years.

For the first time, Scott saw that music was more than pleasant melodies and driving rhythms. Good music had shape and form and style. Jazzed-up versions of church hymns and folk songs made room in the young musician's repertory for sonatas by Mozart and Beethoven. Gradually these three musical sources would come together for the maturing musician to create a new kind of music—rhythmic and exciting and syncopated, but also formal, graceful, and classical. Ragtime.

But before Joplin put it all together, one more ingredient was added to the musical stew. That was the jaunty music being played nightly in the saloons and honky-tonks of Texarkana and a thousand towns like it by wandering musicians, both black and white. They played for money to entertain the customers and then moved on to the next town and its honky-tonks. As the musicians moved from place to place they picked up tunes and techniques from other musicians they befriended. It was a kind of cross-fertilization like that which occurs between bees and flowers, making for new and more beautiful blossoms. And so it was with the music.

Although still a youngster, Scott would go into the honky-tonks and listen, enraptured, to the music these wandering minstrels played. He dreamed of the day he might make his living doing the same.

Like Scott, these black musicians were playing their own souped-up versions of the popular, commercial white music of the day. This included the ever-popular marches of John Philip Sousa, known as "the March King" (1854–1932), and the romantic, sentimental piano music of Louis Moreau Gottschalk (1829–1869). A footnote in American musical history today, in his own time Gottschalk was extremely popular and the first American composer to gain acceptance in Europe. Although his name sounded as German as Beethoven, Gottschalk was actually of Creole descent and was born in New Orleans. A concert pianist, his compositions drew on the rich Creole folk music of his native city as well as Spanish, Latin, and West Indian music. Many of his piano pieces had the sophisticated rhythms and gliding grace that would have as profound an influence on Scott Joplin as the black music he grew up with.

When Scott reached his teens, he began playing at local church functions and socials, gaining a local reputation as a prodigy. At sixteen, he formed his own vocal group with his brothers Willie and Robert and two other friends, Wesley Kirby and Tom Clark. Although they were a quintet, for some reason they called themselves "The Texas Medley Quartette." Scott's singing voice was nearly as good as his piano playing and the Quartette was a popular act at parties and dances. Soon they were traveling to other Texas towns to perform, and then north into Missouri.

Besides playing with the Quartette, Scott performed as a solo pianist at local events. His repertory was impressive, ranging from marches and ballads to popular songs and church music. People seemed to enjoy his playing the most when he "jazzed up" a piece of music, energizing it with complicated African and Latin rhythms.

By the time he was twenty, Scott Joplin was ready to take his music on the road. He felt confident enough to join those itinerant musicians who traveled from town to town playing in saloons for their living. This kind of establishment might not have been his first choice of a venue for his talents, but then he had little choice. The two main options for a black musician who wanted a career were the church or the saloon. In the church, Scott's musical creativity would be severely limited and there was little chance of finding fortune and fame. So he chose the other route. He bid farewell to his mother and siblings and struck out for the open road.

BARROOMS, BORDELLOS, AND BAWDY HOUSES

Many claim to have invented ragtime, just as many claim jazz and blues. But the inventor individuals have been lost in the folk fog of pre-history. You may figure that ragtime was African, an extension of the voodoo thump of the tom-tom, you may claim that it was nothing more than bar-room pianists getting fed-up with churning out the same old pop tunes and jiggling the melodies. You may say anything.[1]

—Ian Whitcomb

As America grew in the post—Civil War period, business and industry boomed. The railroad moved steadily westward, helping to settle the frontier and unite the country. Americans went to work building their nation, and when the long workday was done they had a need for leisure and recreation as never before.

In the West of the 1880s, the saloon, with its impressive bar, gaming tables, and dance-hall girls in frilly dresses, served the needs of dusty cowboys fresh off the trail and other hardworking men. The rest of America had its saloons and honky-tonks to relax in, too. The towns and cities of the East and Midwest, however, were more settled and civilized than the frontier towns, and that created a problem. Respectable citizens didn't want a saloon, gambling hall, or "house of ill repute" next door or just down the street. So the town leaders, in their wisdom, decided that if they couldn't close down these palaces of pleasure and sin, at least they could group them together in one place, a safe distance from where the decent people in town lived.

The owners of these establishments didn't seem to mind this forced segregation. It made it easier for their patrons to find them, and the healthy competition often ended up being good for everyone's business. Thus was brought into being what became known as the "red light district," so called because the houses of prostitution, or brothels and bordellos, advertised themselves with a red light hung at the door or in a window. This part of town was also called the "sporting district" or simply "the district."

Life in the district was loose and easy, occasionally punctuated by violence and crime. The tired boatman and laborer could unwind, for a price, with "wine, women, and song." The saloons provided the wine (although beer and hard liquor were the preferred beverages), the brothels and bordellos provided the women, and itinerant musicians pounding away on upright pianos provided the song.

Music was an integral part of any successful district. It helped to create a carefree, happy atmosphere for the carrying-on of otherwise sordid activities. Although in some houses female dancers danced and stripped to the music, it usually served a less straightforward purpose. The music wasn't so much meant to be listened to as absorbed subliminally—an aural backdrop to such more important activities as drinking, gambling, or choosing a prostitute for the night. It was a kind of early American Muzak.

To provide the music, saloon owners and madames hired professional piano players, both black and white, who would play for a week or two and then move on to the next establishment or town. The pay wasn't much, but a talented musician could often earn big tips from the patrons.

"In those days a good meal cost a quarter and a fine tailor-made suit twenty-five dollars," remembered piano player and composer Sam Patterson. "With ten to twenty a night in tips, a piano player had more than he could spend so long as he didn't gamble or play the ponies. Lots of players didn't even bother to work except when they felt in the mood or needed a few dollars. . . ."[2]

When they didn't find work in honky-tonks, musicians could work at fairs and racetracks. In the heartland, where the Mississippi and other rivers controlled commerce and trade, these musicians, like the dockworkers, river men, and traders who were their customers, were constantly on the move and liked it that way.

It was into this adventurous, rowdy world that Scott Joplin entered sometime in the mid-1880s. His first jobs playing piano may have been on the riverboats, floating pleasure palaces that cruised the Mississippi with passengers and the gamblers and confidence men who preyed on them. Like other musicians, Joplin would eventually get off in a town along the river and check out the district for work. If a job could be found, he'd have steady work for a week or two. When the management hired a new musician, or Joplin became bored with his surroundings, he would hop on board the next river boat and go on to the next town. It was a nomadic life but one that suited a young man who wanted to see the world and learn his craft.

The "circuit" was a small world in which the musicians got to know each other, traded tunes, competed at the keyboard, and picked up new playing techniques from one another. As ragtime historian Rudi Blesh notes, "Drifting

Musicians and other performers were hired to entertain the passengers on the steamboats that traveled up and down the Mississippi River. Scott Joplin probably was one of the many itinerant piano players who found work—and a means of travel—in this thriving business.

from one open town to the next, following the fairs, the races, and the excursions, these men formed a real folk academy."[3]

Young Joplin got an education in this "academy" that no music school in the country could have provided. Like a sponge, he absorbed the styles of the experienced players he met. In the river towns he could hear every kind of music people enjoyed, from the Negro spirituals and hymns of the churches to the marches of the local brass bands to the sentimental ballads played on the parlor pianos. He adapted all of these styles into his own "rag" style, a rich conglomerate of American popular music.

The patchwork nature of the music Joplin and his colleagues played in the districts of the river towns may have led to the music being called "rag." In fact, the sheet music cover of Joplin's first published rag, "Original Rags," pictures an old black man picking rags.

But there are at least two equally plausible explanations for how the term originated. One relates to the instrument generally acknowledged as giving birth to rag music—the banjo. Although ragtime became most closely associated with the piano, it was the peculiar style of banjo playing by blacks in the early 1800s from which the rag style originated. These homespun musicians would pick out a tune on the banjo's strings while stomping their feet to keep the beat. This strong rhythm accompanying a catchy melody was picked up by piano players, who played the rhythm with their left hand and the melody with their right. It is very possible Joplin got this style of playing at an early age listening to his mother play folk tunes on the banjo. This musical style of banjo picking came to be called "ragpicking" when transferred to the piano.

A third explanation for "rag" comes from the musical tempo these musicians played in. As inventive as these men were, they didn't necessarily make up their own music. They took contemporary tunes–ballads, stage songs, marches, and even church hymns–and then added

28

a syncopated beat and upbeat rhythm, making them their own. Syncopation, the shifting of the normal accent by stressing the normally unaccented beats, was integral to this kind of piano playing. The style was first called "jag" or "jig" time, presumably after the jig, a lively dance done in triple time. Eventually, "jig" was changed to "rag," because the musicians rendered the melody line so ragged and broken as to be almost unrecognizable. Interestingly enough, Scott Joplin, whose name would later become synonymous with ragtime music, detested the term and called it "scurrilous."[4]

Sometime in the middle to late 1880s, the young Joplin grew tired of the circuit and settled down in the grandest river town of them all—St. Louis.

Originally a French fur-trading post on the Mississippi, by 1870 St. Louis was the third-largest city in the United States after New York and Philadelphia. Aptly named "the Gateway to the West," St. Louis was the jumping-off place for western exploration and migration ever since Lewis and Clark first left there in 1804 for their historic expedition West to the Pacific. Between 1840 and 1860, St. Louis's population grew ten times over. By 1900 more than 60 percent of the city's population was black. Although as segregated as any other American city in its day, St. Louis had a thriving black middle class, with a number of the establishments in the district owned by blacks.

This district, one of the largest in the Midwest, was located near both the waterfront and the Union Railroad Station in a section of the city known as Chestnut Valley. Here, between Chestnut and Market Streets, Joplin found immediate work in the saloons and bawdy houses.

Although the young black musician worked nightly in these dens of vice, little of their taint rubbed off on him. Unlike many of the local musicians, he dressed conservatively, spoke softly, had good manners and paid more attention to his music than to the whirling life going on around him. His uncanny ability to improvise on the spot

In the late 1800s St. Louis, Missouri, known as the Gateway to the West, was the third-largest city in the United States, with a flourishing musical life in the cafes and bordellos. Pictured is a view of Broadway from Chestnut Street.

with a given tune won him the admiration and respect of musicians twice his age. But Joplin was too serious about his talent to become cocky or egotistical. He kept learning, listening and perfecting his craft. As Peter Gammond writes in his excellent study *Scott Joplin and the Ragtime Era*, in St. Louis Joplin was "not so much studying music as having it poured through his ears and filtered through his brain, at almost every waking hour of the day."[5]

Joplin soon gravitated to one of Chestnut Hill's finest establishments, the Silver Dollar Saloon at 425 South Twelfth Street. The proprietor, "Honest" John L. Turpin, was a former laborer and pianist in his own right who not only made Joplin his regular pianist but adopted him as a member of his family. Turpin had three sons who also aspired to be ragtime musicians, two of whom were, at the time, off mining for silver in Nevada.

People flocked to the Silver Dollar to hear Joplin play. Many of these music lovers were musicians themselves who came to Honest John's to while away the hours talking and playing music in friendly competition while they waited for word of new job openings at other establishments in the district.

Although Joplin enjoyed the stability and financial security of life in St. Louis, he didn't entirely abandon his previous lifestyle. Using St. Louis as his home base, he still went on the road, traveling to other Missouri river towns such as Carthage, Columbia, Sedalia, and Hannibal, boyhood home of America's most popular author, Samuel Clemens, better known as Mark Twain. He even traveled as far as Cincinnati, Ohio, and Louisville, Kentucky, on occasion.

Other than these bare facts, we know precious little about Joplin's life in the seven years or so he spent in St. Louis. What we do know is that he matured from a journeyman musician to a master of his craft. Like many of his fellow musicians, Joplin was a composer who created his own rag music but didn't write a note of it down. All the music these men knew they carried around in their heads. Unlike Joplin, most of them couldn't even read music and had never studied with a teacher.

Although Joplin enjoyed the respect of his peers and the steady money he made playing at the Silver Dollar, his life remained strangely unfulfilled. He wanted to create music that could be appreciated not only by the denizens of St. Louis saloons but by the general public. Joplin wanted to compose like Mozart, Beethoven, and the other masters he had learned about from his classical music teacher. But as a black man in late nineteenth century America this was something he dared not aspire to. The people who controlled the music publishing business were all white. Why would they want to publish the music of a black composer? And even if they did, who in the white middle-class public would buy such music? Scott Joplin put such dreams in the back of his mind and concentrated on his playing.

Then, in 1893, an event took place that would bring his dream back to life. The city of Chicago, Illinois, decided to throw a fair to celebrate the 400th anniversary of the discovery of America by Christopher Columbus. It would be a fair unlike any the world had seen before—the first truly "world's fair." And along with millions of other Americans, Scott Joplin went to see it and find work there as a musician. He would find that and much more.

BIRTH OF
A COMPOSER

[He was] a very black Negro, solidly built, about five feet, seven inches tall; a good dresser, usually neat, but sometimes a little careless with his clothes; gentlemanly and pleasant, with a liking for companionship. . . . he had poise, and a sort of calm determination in the expression, with confidence in his ability to look out for himself.[1]

—Brun Campbell and Roy Carew describing Scott Joplin

"The greatest event in the history of the country since the Civil War,"[2] is how newspaper correspondent Richard Harding Davis described the Columbian Exposition, better known as the Chicago World's Fair of 1893.

Few chose to quarrel with this assessment. Set in the city's Jackson Park on Lake Michigan, the fair was a city within a city. "The White City," as the fairgrounds were called, consisted of neoclassical alabaster buildings and pavilions set off by elegant pools and fountains designed

The Columbian Exposition, better known as the Chicago
World's Fair, was held in 1893 to commemorate
Columbus's arrival in the Americas. Scott Joplin found
opportunity to perform in the fair's sporting district (not
shown in this photo), which ringed the fairgrounds.

by legendary architect Daniel H. Burnham. The various pavilions displayed the scientific, technological, and artistic achievements of the age, showing to the world how far America had progressed in the three decades since the Civil War.

The fair drew an unprecedented 27 million people and had something to interest them all. For the adventurous there was a new circular amusement ride built by Pittsburgh bridge designer, George Washington Gale Ferris. The first Ferris wheel could hold 2,160 people at one time and was ringed by 3,000 light bulbs. For the intellectuals there was the dramatic demonstration of scientist-showman Nikola Tesla, inventor of the alternating current, who stunned crowds when 1,000,000 volts of electric current passed through his body without harming him. For the curiosity seekers there was the fabulous Midway, which boasted escape artist Harry Houdini, exotic belly dancer Little Egypt, the Darling of the Nile; boxing great Gentleman Jim Corbett in exhibition fights; and a two-headed pig.

Yet for all its cultural diversity, the Chicago Fair all but ignored the achievements of African-Americans. The fair's single concession to blacks was a humiliating one. On a special "Colored People's Day," the fair's organizers gave out 2,500 watermelons to the crowds. Distinguished black leader Frederick Douglass was so enraged at the exclusion of his people's accomplishments that he wrote and distributed a broadside to fairgoers entitled "The Reason Why the Colored American Is Not in the World's Columbian Exposition."[3]

Black performers were welcome, however, in the fair's sporting district, which ringed the fairgrounds. It was here that ragtime musicians played in the same type of honky-tonks and saloons they had always played in. But this particular district was special in that it attracted the top musicians from across the Midwest. The irresistible rhythm of ragtime attracted black and white patrons from all over the

Black performers were breaking into vaudeville and changing musical tastes by the turn of the century.

United States and Europe who stopped by the district for a relaxing respite from all that progress and culture.

It was an exciting time in the musical history of America and twenty-five-year-old Scott Joplin was right in the middle of it—playing and learning new techniques from such legendary Chicago piano players as "Plunk" Henry Johnson and Johnny Seymour, whose bar was one of the most popular ragtime joints in the district.

Black music was pervasive at the fair and it wasn't all ragtime. The musical play *The Creole Show*, packed one fairground theater for a full season and was the first black musical that did not rely on the crude humor and blackface of the old minstrel shows. The racist coon jokes, sketches, and songs of the minstrel shows had been an entertainment staple form since the 1840s. It was now being replaced by entertainments that took blacks seriously and allowed them to portray themselves onstage, instead of having whites in blackface play them. Shows such as *The Creole Show* featured the singing, dancing, and musicianship of talented black performers who didn't act stupid or shuffle and scratch their heads.

Another show Joplin probably saw at the fair was *Mahara's Minstrels*, written by black composer W. C. Handy, who would later claim the title of "father of the blues." Handy's show drew on the rich musical heritage of the deep South, never before heard on a legitimate stage.

These stage shows incorporating black music excited Joplin and opened up a whole world of possibilities to him. For the first time, he saw popular black music existing outside of the smoky atmosphere of a saloon or honky-tonk and in a real theater where paying customers—both black and white—came to listen and be entertained.

Just how Joplin spent his time in the months he stayed at the fair when he wasn't playing piano is not known. But he did make a new friend who would play an important role in his future. Otis Saunders, two years younger than Joplin, was a ragtime pianist from Springfield, Missouri.

Scott Joplin's piano

Nicknamed "Crackerjack," Saunders was so light-skinned that some people considered him a white man. Saunders became Joplin's closest companion in Chicago.

Like the other serious musicians Joplin met, Saunders recognized his musical gifts and knew that those gifts would be largely wasted unless Joplin began putting down his compositions on paper and found a publisher for them. What seemed like a distant dream for the young musician only a year or two earlier now seemed much less so. If W. C. Handy—a black man and three years Joplin's junior—could write a hit musical, why couldn't Joplin publish his own distinctive music?

Joplin's first step in this direction was to form his own instrumental band. Brass bands were extremely popular in the era of John Philip Sousa, and Joplin's band gave him the invaluable experience of creating his own orchestrations for the group. The ensemble consisted of cornet, clarinet, tuba, and baritone horn. Joplin, the group leader, played cornet and piano. Playing with his own band at the fair was fun, but by early 1894 Joplin decided it was time to take what he had learned back to his old stomping grounds in St. Louis.

Accompanied by Otis Saunders, Joplin left Chicago in early 1894 and made his way slowly west to St. Louis, playing honky-tonks along the way to pay for the journey. The musicians were in no hurry and didn't arrive in St. Louis until nearly a year later.

In the several years Joplin had been away, there had been some changes in Chestnut Hill. Two of John Turpin's sons—Tom and Charlie—had returned from a mining venture in Nevada in 1894. Tom was running a new restaurant his father had opened at 2222 Market Street called the Rosebud Bar. Like Scott and Otis, Tom Turpin was a ragtime enthusiast and a budding composer. He had begun to write down his own rag compositions and urged Joplin to do the same.

Within a short time, Joplin and Saunders decided to leave St. Louis for the nearby small city of Sedalia,

Missouri. Sedalia was a less hectic place than St. Louis and better suited the serious-minded Joplin. It also had one of the biggest and most flourishing sporting districts in the Midwest, where the two young musicians could be assured of finding steady work.

Although he went back to playing piano in honky-tonks, Joplin continued to expand his musical horizons. He joined the all-black Queen City Concert Band in Sedalia, playing second cornet. This twelve-man ensemble was one of the best known in the region and played marches, popular songs, and the new black dance that was beginning to sweep the nation—the cakewalk.

The popularity of the cakewalk paralleled that of ragtime music. The cakewalk's history, notes Peter Gammond, "is so intertwined with ragtime that it is often difficult to untangle them."[4]

The cakewalk supposedly started out when African-Americans in the deep South imitated the dances of the Seminole Indians, who alternated frenetic jumping with a slow processional march. Blacks turned the Indian jump-march into an almost cartoon-like strut that poked fun at the pretensions of white society. It turned the tables on the white performers who had imitated blacks for decades in the minstrel shows.

From Florida, the cakewalk spread north, eventually reaching New York City. Cakewalk clubs were founded and sponsored dance contests. The winners were given large, decorated cakes, which is probably where the name "cakewalk" and the expression "That takes the cake" originated. The winners were expected to cut the cake and share it with the other dancers.

While Joplin enjoyed playing with the Queen City Band, he wanted to have his own band again. He left the ensemble and re-formed the Texas Medley Quartette with his brothers Will and Robert, who had recently joined him in Sedalia. Originally a vocal group, they now added instruments to their ensemble and grew to an octet. Joplin was leader, conductor, and soloist of the group and arranged all their music. He also began composing music for the group. Oscar Dame of St. Louis and the Majestic Booking Agency sponsored the group to go on tour.

Joplin's first compositions were not the rags he later perfected in the Silver Dollar Saloon and other establishments, but more conventional songs that were popular at the time. His first two efforts, "A Picture of Her Face" and "Please Say You Will," were nearly indistinguishable from hundreds of other sentimental ballads of the day and showed none of the promise of what was to come. Perhaps at the time Joplin lacked confidence and felt on firmer ground writing music that was already commercially successful.

This excerpt from the lyric of "A Picture of Her Face," shows that music, and not words, was Joplin's strength as an artist.

> I've yet a treasure in this world
> A picture of her face,
> It brings joy to me when ofttimes sad at heart.
> Her picture I can see and sad thoughts then depart.
> Although my love is dead, my only darling Grace,
> My eyes are ofttimes looking on
> A picture of—her—face.[5]

While on tour in upstate New York, Joplin submitted the two songs to several music publishers in Syracuse. Leiter Brothers, owners of a music store, bought and published "A Picture of Her Face" and M. L. Montell accepted "Please Say You Will." Both pieces made barely a ripple on the sheet-music sales chart but gave Joplin his start as a published composer.

His next efforts were three piano solo pieces in a more classical vein. Two of them, "Combination March" and "Harmony Club Waltz," were pleasant enough and showed the influence of ragtime but were otherwise not remarkable. However, the third composition, "The Great Crash Collision March," was strikingly original. A kind of tone poem, the composition was a stirring reenactment of a train wreck, humorously dedicated to the Missouri, Kansas, and Texas Railroad. Rudi Blesh considers "The Great Crash Collision March" to be "more of a descriptive overture than a march." The parts of the piece are given descriptive titles, a device that Joplin rarely used in his later compositions: "The noise of the trains while running at the rate of sixty miles per hour," "Whistling for the crossing," "The train noise," "Whistling before the collision," and "The collision."[6]

All three of these piano pieces were published in Temple, Texas, another stop for the Texas Medley Octet on their second tour. The tour ended, appropriately enough, in Joplin, Missouri (not named for the composer), where Joplin disbanded the group. Perhaps he was tired of playing on the road and wanted more time to devote to composing. In any event, Joplin decided to settle down again and in mid-1896 moved back to Sedalia. Here he could play piano nightly in the district and have his days free to compose. He didn't know it yet, but in Sedalia he would find the success as a composer that he had been searching for.

THE ENTERTAINER

*Will give a good time, for instance Master Scott
Joplin, the entertainer. . . .*[1]

*—back of business card for the Maple Leaf
Club, c. 1899*

When Scott Joplin arrived in Sedalia, Missouri, the
city had a reputation of being one of the least racist
communities in the South. Blacks made up nearly
half the population and first settled there to work in the pro-
cessing, packing, and shipping businesses. It wasn't long
before some blacks were running their own businesses,
including a number of saloons and honky-tonks in
Sedalia's thriving red-light district.

The town was founded by General George R. Smith,
who in 1859 purchased a thousand acres of prime farm-
land on the rolling prairie 96 miles east of Kansas City.
Smith made his farm the hub of a small community he
called Sedville, after his beloved daughter Sarah, whose
nickname was Sed. With the coming of the railroad, little
Sedville grew into the town of Sedalia. By the 1890s it

had a population of fifteen thousand. Sedalia was important enough to be considered a potential state capital. Instead, it became the county seat of Pettis County.

But what most attracted Scott Joplin to Sedalia was the George R. Smith College for Negroes, one of the first colleges for African-Americans established in the north. It was founded by Sarah Smith as a memorial for her father and had an excellent music department. The curriculum included courses in how to play musical instruments from the piano to the mandolin. But what most interested Joplin were courses in musical theory, orchestration, and composition.

If he was to develop and grow as a composer, Joplin needed to learn how to transfer the joyful, energetic music that pulsated from his fingertips into tiny black notes on a sheet of music paper. He took composition and other courses at the college during the day and played piano in the district at night to pay for his tuition and living expenses.

Of Sedalia's more than thirty saloons, the two most prominent were the Black 400 Club and the Maple Leaf Club. Joplin first got a job at the Black 400 Club, but it wasn't long before he was hired by Will and Walker Williams to play at the Maple Leaf. The Williams brothers hired Joplin at the urging of Otis Saunders, Joplin's unofficial promoter and agent. Once they heard Joplin's graceful playing and saw the many customers who flocked to hear him, the Williamses were ready to make him their "resident professor."

Playing at the Maple Leaf Club not only provided Joplin with financial security but also allowed him to pursue his first love—composing. In the afternoons, business was slow and he could sit undisturbed at the piano and compose new rags. It was the support and encouragement of the Williams brothers that led Joplin to name one of his first and most famous rags in their honor—the "Maple Leaf Rag."

In addition to his busy schedule of school, piano playing, and composing, Joplin soon added a fourth activity—teaching. As ragtime's popularity spread, many young black men wanted to learn how to play this difficult new music. Older, more traditional music teachers refused to learn ragtime or teach it to others. Their attitude toward this new music can be best summed up in these comments from piano teacher Philip Gordon writing in the *Musical Observer*: "Ragtime will ruin your touch, disable your technic, misuse your knowledge of pedaling, and pervert whatever sense of poetry and feeling you have into superficial, improper channels. Shun it as you would the 'Black Death.'"[2]

But many embraced it and Scott Joplin found students pounding his door, eager to learn his technique of playing. One of his first pupils was Arthur Marshall, a fellow student at George Smith College. Marshall was a local Sedalia boy, thirteen years Joplin's junior. Despite the age difference, the two became close friends; Joplin lived his first five or six months in Sedalia in the home of Marshall's parents, where he rented a room.

Although he could be remote and reserved, Joplin loved people, particularly other musicians. He was a giving, generous teacher and friend. His friendships with Marshall and another talented student, Scott Hayden, would soon blossom into a number of rich musical collaborations. Together these three, with two other gifted composers, would form the core of the classical rag movement. Joplin would be a friend, supporter, and tremendous influence on all of them.

Not all Joplin's students were black. Brun Campbell, a young white man from Kansas, arrived in Sedalia after the success of the "Maple Leaf Rag" and was introduced to Joplin by Otis Saunders. After listening to Campbell play, Joplin was impressed enough to take him on as a student. Campbell, who wrote about his experiences with Joplin in 1952, had this to say about his famous teacher:

Scott Joplin named me the "Ragtime Kid" after he had taught me to play his first four rags, and as I was leaving him and Sedalia to return to my home in Kansas he gave me a bright, new, shiny half dollar and called my attention to the date on it. "Kid," he said, "This half dollar is dated 1897, the year I wrote my first rag. Carry it for good luck and as you go through life it will always be a reminder of your early ragtime days here at Sedalia." There was a strange look in his eyes which I shall never forget.[3]

By 1898, Joplin had completed the composition of two rags, "Maple Leaf Rag" and "Original Rags," and was ready to start looking for a publisher. Sedalia had two music publishers—Stark and Son and A.W. Perry and Sons. Because Stark had a reputation for publishing weepy ballads, Joplin felt he stood a better chance with Perry. But Perry wasn't interested in Joplin's rags, probably for the same reason Stark was initially reluctant to publish them—their high degree of difficulty for the average amateur player. Rudi Blesh and Harriet Janis believe Perry might have published "Maple Leaf Rag" if Joplin had agreed to change the title. Perry had already published a "Maple Leaf Waltz" by composer Florence Johnson and may have felt the similarity of the titles would confuse his customers. But Joplin, out of loyalty to the Williams brothers, would not change the title.

Joplin next took his compositions to Carl Hoffman, a bigger publisher, in Kansas City. Ironically, Hoffman liked "Original Rags" and agreed to publish it but turned down "Maple Leaf."

Peter Gammond, Joplin's first biographer, has called "Original Rags" "a fascinating debut for a ragtime composer [that] stands among Joplin's best works."[4] Like other early Joplin rags, "Original Rags" is happy and upbeat. Its classical form was carefully structured in five themes.

The piece begins with a brief introduction and then goes into the first theme, or strain: a jaunty, upbeat little tune. The melody is repeated once, and then a second theme in the same key as the first is played and repeated. A third theme emerges in a new key and is played twice. It is less rhythmic than the first two and more melodic. After the third section, the opening theme is played through again, followed by a fourth theme in the original key. In most later rags, the fourth theme ends the composition, but in "Original Rags" Joplin introduced a fifth theme. He later realized that this fifth theme was unnecessary and that four were enough. This structure of four themes was the model for most future rags. Joplin may also have been influenced by the four movements of the classical symphony and sonata.

The first three sections of "Original Rags" have an infectious bounce and gracious charm that would be a hallmark of nearly all Joplin's rags. The mood is not sustained, however, and the last two sections are weaker and less inventive, ending the rag on a somewhat unsatisfying note.

The title credits on the sheet music of "Original Rags" has raised some questions about its originality. The credit reads "picked by Scott Joplin; arranged by Chas. N. Daniels." To reinforce the ragpicking analogy, as noted earlier, the sheet-music cover illustration shows an old Negro picking up rags in front of a run-down shack. It is possible Joplin "picked" the rag themes from traditional rags he heard other musicians play on the circuit and gave them to Daniels, a composer in his own right, to arrange. But it is just as possible, that Daniels, who was white and later wrote the hit song "Hiawatha" (1901), may have merely helped Joplin get the rag accepted for publication by lending his name to it. Once his reputation was established, Joplin himself did this favor for other composers.

Whatever its history, "Original Rags" was not the first published piano rag. That honor goes to "Louisiana Rag," by Theo Northrup. "Mississippi Rag," a cakewalk written by white band leader William Krell, appeared in late 1897 and was the first composition to use the word rag in its title. This was followed by "Harlem Rag" (1898), written by Joplin's old friend Tom Turpin and the first rag published by an African-American. None of these compositions, however, approaches the grace, style, and finish of Joplin's "Original Rags," which first appeared in 1899.

But it was the release of "Maple Leaf Rag" later that same year that revealed the true dimension of Joplin's talents. Joplin himself knew the importance of this rag, for he confided to Arthur Marshall that "one day the 'Maple Leaf' will make me king of ragtime composers."[5]

When most people think of ragtime, they think of the "Maple Leaf Rag"—and for good reason. In this composition Joplin captured forever the pure joy and jaunty confidence of the ragtime era, one that would dominate American popular music for nearly two decades. One can hear in its bouncy strains all the honky-tonks, saloons, and bordellos Joplin ever played in. It is almost impossible to listen to "Maple Leaf Rag" and not move some part of your body to its infectious beat. Its rhythmic drive and sprightly melodies are irresistible. "The first strain is a miracle of perfection," writes Peter Gammond, "an inspirational phenomenon, harmonically sophisticated yet completely uncontrived."[6] Yet what is so remarkable is that the high peak reached in this first section never falters. Each of the following three themes are uniquely exciting, yet are all derived from the same musical language. The last strain sums up all that has gone before in a breathless finish to a composition that is quintessential ragtime. Although Joplin would go on to write rags with a far wider emotional range, greater subtlety, and a more intense personal lyricism, he would never top "Maple Leaf Rag" for pure musical exuberance.

The Chicago World's Fair brought ragtime music to the attention of the American public, but it took the phenomenal success of "Maple Leaf Rag" to make ragtime the rage of a nation. It became the first truly American music, combining European form with the dynamic drive and rhythms of black and white American folk music.

Ragtime, like jazz in the 1920s and rock and roll in the 1950s and 1960s, was a music that reflected its times. The "Gay Nineties" were giving way to the first decade of the twentieth century. Inventors such as Thomas Edison and the Wright brothers were changing the world Americans lived in. The United States victory in the Spanish-American War of 1898 helped transform the nation into a world power. It was an exciting time to be an American and ragtime captured the vibrancy and optimism of the period.

As writer and musician Ian Whitcomb observes:

> *Ragtime was more than a music. It was Our Time—the ragtime life with patent leather shoes in many colors plus pearl buttons, a soft shirt of loud silk; female secretaries grabbing the snatched lunch, gobbling an evening meal made by just adding heat; all living on hot asphalt surrounded by autos, phonographs, movies and all part of a wide world which exploded daily in banner headlines. . . .*[7]

While ragtime had its millions of enthusiasts, its sudden popularity brought on a storm of criticism as well. Among the most vocal and virulent attacks were those from members of the musical establishment, for which the only good music was that of the classical European masters of the nineteenth century. While this music was truly great, many of the contemporary composers of classical music, particularly in America, were second-raters. Culture in the United States was still largely derived from Europe. Classical music was largely superimposed on American society and many upper- and middle-class urban Americans attended concerts and the opera less out of love for the music than because they were "supposed" to. The stagnant quality of much serious music in this country may help explain why so many people were attracted to the vitality and freshness of ragtime.

The harsh attacks on ragtime, such as this one from the journal *Musical Courier*, are surprisingly similar to attacks made over half a century later on another genre of popular music—rock and roll:

> *A wave of vulgar, filthy, and suggestive music has inundated the land. The pabulum of theatre and summer hotel orchestras is coon music. Nothing but ragtime prevails and the cakewalk with its obscene posturing, its lewd gestures. It is artistically and morally depressing and should be suppressed by press and pulpit.*[8]

The reasons ragtime inspired such hatred go far beyond the music itself. A not-so-subtle racism was at work here as well. Both ragtime and the cakewalk dance that inspired it were originally played and performed almost exclusively by black people. "Ragtime is a term applied to the peculiar, broken, rhythmic features of the popular `coon song,'" writes another critic. "It has a powerfully stimulating effect, setting the nerves and muscles tingling with excitement. Its aesthetic element is the same as that in the monotonous, recurring rhythmic chant of barbarous races."[9] This kind of undisguised racism reflected a society that created Jim Crow laws to segregate blacks from whites in every area of daily life.

A third reason for the attacks on ragtime was its place of origin, the saloons, brothels, and gambling halls of America. "How could any good music arise from such dens of iniquity?" clergy across the nation asked their congregations. Ragtime was the devil's music and could only lead those who listened to it, particularly the young and impressionable, down the road to ruin.

"In Christian homes, where purity and morals are stressed, ragtime should find no resting place," wrote Leo Oehmler in the *Musical Observer*. "Avaunt the ragtime rot! Let us purge America and the Divine Art of Music from this polluting nuisance."[10]

It didn't matter to many upright Christians that, thanks to the "Maple Leaf Rag," ragtime could be heard being played in middle-class parlors in every city and town by proper young men and women, most of them white. This very idea alarmed many upright citizens, such as the writer in the musical journal *Étude* who wrote: "The counters of the music stores are loaded with this virulent poison, which in the form of a malarious epidemic, is finding its way into the homes and brains of youth."[11]

But like rock and roll, the popularity of ragtime could not be stemmed by its critics. Ragtime had arrived at just the right moment in American cultural history. The birth of the player piano, the phonograph, and the new affordability of such former luxuries as a piano in the home made it the first fad to fully benefit from the new popular culture of the middle class.

Like his music, Scott Joplin himself had made the leap to respectability. The royalties he earned from sales of his famous rag allowed him to finally pack in his piano and leave the saloon for his study, where he could compose ragtime instead of only playing it. Although he continued to perform at the Maple Leaf Club, it was now as a visiting celebrity and not the resident professor.

Even as the "Maple Leaf Rag" was hitting the music stands, Joplin was busy at work writing new rags with Arthur Marshall and Scott Hayden. During the summer of 1899 he wrote "Swipesy" with Marshall, which is subtitled a cakewalk. This slow rag was adequate but had none of the originality of "Maple Leaf," possibly because

The introduction of the player piano increased the demand for piano music such as the piano rags.

it wasn't 100 percent Joplin. Perhaps what is most intriguing about "Swipesy" is its title. John Stark had a neighborhood shoe shine boy pose for a photograph for the sheet music cover. The boy's hanging head suggested to Marshall a guilty conscience, as if he had just swiped some cookies. Hence, the title "Swipesy."

Stark, now settled in his new offices in St. Louis, invited Joplin to join him there. But Scott had entered into another kind of collaboration that kept him in Sedalia. Scott Hayden had a sister-in-law, a pretty young widow named Belle. Joplin, who rented a room in the Hayden household after leaving the Marshalls, was smitten with Belle and the two were soon engaged. About the same time, Joplin met Alfred Ernst, the German-born director of the St. Louis Choral Symphony Society. Ernst was one classicist who appreciated Joplin's music and saw the tremendous potential of ragtime. He reawakened Joplin's love of classical music and encouraged him to extend himself in classical forms. He later invited the young black composer to accompany him to Germany to study and perform, a trip that it is unlikely Joplin ever made.

Sometime in 1900 Belle Hayden and Joplin may have married. A short time later they moved to St. Louis where the composer could study with Ernst and continue to write rags for Stark's growing publishing house. The entertainer had hung up his hat and was ready to leave the place in which he had experienced his initial success. Scott Joplin's dream of becoming a great composer was beginning to become reality.

S / X

KING OF RAGTIME

Despite the ebony hue of his features and a retiring disposition [Joplin] has written probably more instrumental successes than any other local composer.[1]

—the St. Louis Globe-Democrat

Scott Joplin left St. Louis a journeyman musician and returned seven years later one of the most celebrated composers in America. He settled down with his new wife in a respectable neighborhood at 2658A Morgan Street in a house bought with royalties from "Maple Leaf Rag." In a short time they were joined by Scott Hayden and his new bride, Nora Wright, who lived with the Joplins for a time. Arthur Marshall and Otis Saunders, who was traveling with a minstrel troupe, also followed Joplin to St. Louis.

Joplin started to teach piano again, taking on children as well as adults as pupils. To supplement their income from Scott's teaching and composing, Belle turned their home into a boardinghouse, not an uncommon practice among middle-class black and white home owners at that time.

These years in St. Louis would be the most productive of Joplin's career. Over the next seven years he wrote a total of twenty rags, many of them of outstanding quality. He also wrote a score of waltzes, songs, and other piano pieces. In 1901, Joplin's first year in St. Louis, Stark published three of his rags and a waltz. "Peacherine Rag" was the first of Joplin's rags from the plant kingdom, if one discounts "Maple Leaf Rag"—which, after all, was named for a club. In the years ahead would come such rags as "Weeping Willow," "Palm Leaf Rag," "The Sycamore," "Gladiolus Rag," "Rose Leaf Rag," "Heliotrope Bouquet," "Fig Leaf Rag," "Sugar Cane," and "Pine-apple Rag." What attracted Joplin and other rag composers to use so many fruits, flowers, and trees in their titles has never been satisfactorily explained.

The "Peacherine Rag," aside from its jaunty first strain, is not an exceptional rag, but John Stark, ever the enterprising publisher, chose to print the words "by Scott Joplin, the King of the Ragtime Composers" on the sheet music cover. It was a title that would stick.

"Sunflower Slow Drag," Joplin's first collaboration with the talented Scott Hayden, was a much better rag and caused Stark to wax poetic on its composition. He claimed Joplin wrote it "during the high temperature of courtship . . . while he was touching the ground only in the highest places, his geese were all swans, and the Mississippi water tasted like honeydew. . . ."[2]

Stark was apparently less enthusiastic about "The Easy Winners," which he didn't publish (Joplin published it himself). It is possible Stark didn't like this rag because its title alluded to horse racing and gambling, neither of which the straitlaced publisher approved of. The rag itself flows along with an effortless grace, displaying one of the most distinctive characteristics of Joplin's music.

But the virtues of these three rags were overshadowed by "The Entertainer" (1902)—which, after "Maple Leaf Rag," is probably the best-known Joplin rag today, largely

The sheet music cover of Scott Joplin's ragtime
composition "The Entertainer"

due to its use as a theme song in the popular 1973 movie *The Sting*. The rag's title refers to the composer himself, who was given this honorable title at the Maple Leaf Club. Interestingly enough, however, the rag is dedicated to James Brown and his Mandolin Club. Several rag scholars believe the unusual octave chords so distinctive in the rag's first theme were meant to imitate the mandolin's chording.

"The Entertainer," unlike "Maple Leaf Rag," is a slow, easygoing rag with a quiet, folklike style that is completely captivating. It retains the brightness and sunny mood of its predecessors until the last strain, when a tinge of melancholy enters in the form of a minor chord. This reveals a more reflective, thoughtful side of the composer, one that would be more fully explored in the rags of his middle and late period.

But there was an even more serious side of Joplin that was vying with the commercial craft of catchy rags. Before he left Sedalia, probably near the end of 1899, Joplin created a dance piece he called *The Ragtime Dance*, a kind of folk ballet. Unlike his piano rags, this ambitious, twenty-minute piece of music was not meant to be merely played on the piano but performed by a group of dancers on stage. A song-narrator sang along and described each dance as it was performed. *The Ragtime Dance* included many of the popular black social dances of the day, including the cakewalk, the slow drag, the back-step prance, the Jenny Cooler dance, the Sedidus walk, and something called the clean-up.

The narration was the piece's weakest element, again showing Joplin's flaws as a lyricist. Here is a sample:

> Let me see you do the "rag time dance,"
> Turn left and do the "cake walk prance,"
> Turn the other way and do the "slow drag"
> Now take your body to the World's Fair
> And do the "rag time dance."[3]

When Joplin showed his ballet to Stark, the publisher balked. Ragtime meant catchy, tuneful piano compositions, not extended, highbrow stage extravaganzas. If he agreed to publish such an unwieldy work as Joplin's ballet, who would buy it? To convince Stark of the piece's commercial possibilities, Joplin decided to put together a live performance himself. He formed his own dramatic company, rented the Woods Opera House in Sedalia, and put on a full performance of *The Ragtime Dance* for an invited audience. The cast consisted of four dancers; his brother Will Joplin, who sang the libretto, or text; and Joplin himself, who played the piano and led a small orchestra. Stark and his family were in the audience. Arthur Marshall, who helped copy out the orchestra parts, claimed the performance was well received, but Stark was not convinced of its commercial prospects and still refused to publish it.

Joplin put aside his ragtime ballet and returned to writing rags. But he didn't forget *The Ragtime Dance*. After he moved to St. Louis he did more work on it and arranged a second performance. This time he found a strong ally in Stark's daughter Nell, who attended the performance with her father. Nell had just returned from Europe, where she had studied classical music. She was excited and enthusiastic about Joplin's attempt to merge popular music with a classical form, the ballet, and urged her father to publish it. Stark was still unsure. He was a man of discerning taste in music, but he was also a businessperson. He told Joplin that no one would buy such a work—if for no other reason than it would be far longer than the standard piece of sheet music and too expensive.

The two men's disagreement over *The Ragtime Dance* led to the first serious rift in their relationship. Joplin's decision to publish "The Easy Winners" himself may have been his way of getting back at Stark for not publishing his ballet. His next two works, a minstrel song for barbershop-quartet singing with the questionable title "I Am Thinking of

My Pickaninny* Days" and a march, "Cleopha," were published by two other St. Louis publishers.

Anxious to get Joplin back into his stable and perhaps feeling he owed him a favor for establishing his career as a publisher with "Maple Leaf Rag," Stark finally, but reluctantly, agreed to publish *The Ragtime Dance*. The nine-page sheet music was expensive to produce, and as Stark predicted, it sold few copies. But if Stark thought this failure would end Joplin's classical ambitions, he was very much mistaken.

"Joplin's ambition is to shine in other spheres," wrote New York journalist Monroe H. Rosenfeld in an interview with the composer that appeared in the *St. Louis Globe Democrat* around 1903. "To this end he is assiduously toiling upon an opera, nearly a score of the numbers of which he has already composed and which he hopes to give an early production in this city."[4]

The work in question was *A Guest of Honor*, subtitled *A Ragtime Opera*. This one-act opera contained at least a dozen musical numbers. To dance and instrumental and vocal music, Joplin now added drama.

Opera is the unique wedding of music and drama in which the characters sing, rather than speak, their lines. Since its birth in the late 1500s, opera was primarily a classical form and had rarely employed popular music.

When Joplin showed his completed work to Stark, the reaction was predictable. Still smarting from the financial failure of *The Ragtime Dance*, Stark had no intention of publishing a grander work that would sell even fewer copies. When Joplin pressured him to consider it, Stark weakened a bit and said he might take a second look if Joplin could come up with a stronger libretto for his opera. Joplin was not to be dissuaded and once again decided to stage the work himself for Stark to see. This time, however, he didn't

"Pickaninny" is an offensive term for a black child. It was once commonly used in the South.

attempt a full production, which would have been extremely costly, but put on a sort of dress rehearsal in a St. Louis dance hall with his own "Scott Joplin Dramatic Company." Arthur Marshall, who probably helped write out the orchestral parts, claimed years later that the performance "was taken quite well."[5] A theater-circuit manager expressed interest in producing A Guest of Honor but nothing came of it. Another rehearsal performance took place some time later in Sedalia, and Joplin may even have toured the production locally in Missouri and neighboring states for a time. Stark, however, still refused to publish the work.

What the merits of Joplin's first opera were may never be known, for the score and libretto of A Guest of Honor have disappeared without a trace. The opera remains one of the most tantalizing lost works in the history of American music.

What happened to it? Joplin apparently applied for a copyright for his opera and sent a copy to the Copyright Office in Washington, D.C. in early 1903. A card in the office's files refers to "A Guest of Honor, a ragtime opera written and composed by Scott Joplin" but notes that "Copies [were] never received."[6]

If the manuscript was somehow lost in the mail, it seems hard to believe that Joplin wouldn't have retained at least one copy. Some scholars theorize that he became depressed by his failure to get a producer or publisher interested in his opera and destroyed all remaining copies. This seems out of character for a man who would go to any lengths to get his music performed. A better explanation was given by Joplin's second wife, Lottie Stokes, who believed he left the score in a trunk at a Pittsburgh boardinghouse in 1907 or 1908 in lieu of payment while he was performing on the vaudeville circuit. The trunk either disappeared or was never reclaimed by the composer. Sadly, for Joplin scholars, the trunk contained not only A Guest of Honor but a treasure trove of letters, manuscripts, and other personal papers that might have shed invaluable light on the composer's life.

Ragtime enthusiasts retain a slim hope that someday, somewhere, in a dusty desk drawer or in some forgotten attic, a copy of *A Guest of Honor* will turn up and settle one of ragtime's most intriguing mysteries.

Stark's refusal to publish *A Guest of Honor* caused the rift between composer and publisher to widen. Of the nine works Joplin published in 1903 and 1904, only three bear the Stark and Son imprint. The other six were published by two publishers in St. Louis and Chicago. Joplin even sold one rag to Stark's competitor back in Sedalia, A. W. Perry and Sons, the people who originally turned down the "Maple Leaf Rag."

The most noteworthy of these compositions are "Weeping Willow," a quiet rag similar to "The Entertainer" that has as captivating a first theme as Joplin ever wrote; and "The Cascades," one of Joplin's finest achievements. This superb rag is one of the few programmatic pieces that Joplin wrote. As in "The Crush Collision March," the composer skillfully suggests in music an event or thing in the real world.

In 1904 St. Louis had a world's fair to rival the one held in Chicago eleven years earlier. One of the central attractions of the fair was the Cascades Gardens, a stunning combination of waterfalls, lakes, and fountains. Joplin's rag was inspired by the flowing waters of the Gardens and recreated their sublime beauty in cascading notes, most notably in the rag's second section. Like "Maple Leaf Rag" and "The Entertainer," "The Cascades" is an almost flawless composition that moves from strength to strength with grace and ease. To this day it remains one of Joplin's most performed rags.

This was Joplin's first collaboration with Stark in two years, and the publisher publicized it to the hilt, proudly announcing on the cover of the sheet music that it was "The Masterpiece of Scott Joplin." According to rag historians

A vaudeville team of the 1900s,
Bert Williams and George Walker

David A. Jasen and Trebor Jay Tichenor, beginning with "The Cascades" Joplin displayed a "bolder use of the piano's total resources and his rags become more thickly textured."[7]

Despite his failure to attract the public to his experiments in "highbrow" music, Joplin had proved himself to be a serious composer of what Stark ambitiously called "classic ragtime." Stark had invented the term to describe the graceful piano rags of Joplin and his disciples Marshall and Hayden and another rag composer who Stark began publishing, the very talented James Scott. The name differentiated their rags from those more commercial rags being published elsewhere in the country, many of which were not piano rags in the Joplin style but songs written for piano and voice.

But while his professional life was flourishing, Joplin's private life was gradually falling apart. Like the great American composer to precede him, Stephen Foster, Scott Joplin had not married wisely. Foster's wife Jane, for whom he wrote "Jeannie with the Light Brown Hair," had appreciation for neither music nor her husband's ambitions and eventually left him. Belle Hayden was cut from the same cloth. At first, her love for Scott overcame her lack of interest in his profession. But as time went on, she grew tired of the stream of students going through her house and the constant sound of piano playing as her husband taught and composed. Aware of his wife's dissatisfaction, Scott tried to help her appreciate the joys of music. He gave her lessons on the violin, the instrument his father played, but she lacked the temperament and the discipline to master it.

The failure to teach his wife music "seriously humiliated" Joplin, according to Arthur Marshall. "Of course unpleasant attitudes and lack of home interests occurred between them. . . . [Joplin] told me his wife had no interest in his musical career. Otherwise Mrs. Joplin was very pleasant to his friends and especially to we home boys. . . ."[8]

Then Belle discovered she was pregnant. As in many failing marriages, both partners desperately hoped that a child would save the relationship. The little girl was born in early 1903, but her health was poor and she died within a few months. Both Belle and Scott were devastated, but instead of drawing them closer together, their grief only pushed them further apart. They talked of separation, but Scott tried to salvage what was left of their marriage. As Arthur Marshall noted: "Joplin often ordered us to console Mrs. Joplin—perhaps she would reconsider. But she remained neutral. She was never harsh with us, but we just couldn't get her to see the point. So a separation finally resulted."[9]

The failure of his marriage was a crushing blow to the 36-year-old composer. Always an individual of deep traditional values, Joplin longed to have the happy domestic life that would give him the peace and security he needed to create his music. After years of a nomadic life drifting from one town to another, he finally found it, only to have his happiness turned to ashes.

He stayed in St. Louis for a time, exactly how long after splitting with Belle we don't know. But by sometime in 1905 or 1906 Joplin sold a thirteen-room house at 2117 Lucas Avenue to his friend Arthur Marshall, who turned it into a full-time boardinghouse. Joplin then left St. Louis and went back to the open road. He had once been happy and carefree moving from place to place, the only constant in his life being his music. Perhaps he could be happy again on the road and forget his grief.

Of the compositions he wrote in his last year in St. Louis the most extraordinary is "Bethena," a waltz set to a ragtime beat, perhaps the first union of these two musical styles. The first strain of the piece is ravishingly beautiful, one of the most unforgettable melodies Joplin even penned. There is something sublimely fragile and haunting about "Bethena." It is the lonely dance of a man whose heart has been broken.

BACK ON THE ROAD

King of Ragtime Composers—Author of "Maple Leaf Rag"[1]

—Joplin's billing on the vaudeville circuit

The effect of Scott Joplin's failed marriage on his work can be seen dramatically in the sharp decrease in his musical output. From 1899 to 1905 he published seventeen rags and one intermezzo, four songs, three marches, and two waltzes. In 1906, the year of his separation, he turned out only two works. One was a reworking of *The Ragtime Dance* into a conventional rag. The other was "Antoinette," a rather uninspired march with just a tinge of ragtime that might have been penned by Sousa on an off day.

One of Joplin's first stops on the road was Chicago where he lived for a time with Arthur Marshall and his wife. The Marshalls had moved there after selling the Joplin house in St. Louis. In Chicago, Joplin visited Louis Chauvin, a gifted ragtime musician he'd known in St. Louis, who'd fallen on hard times. If Joplin was "King of

Ragtime Composers," Chauvin, thirteen years his junior, was known as "King of Ragtime Players." He had earned the title after winning a ragtime playing contest at the St. Louis World's Fair in 1904. A brilliant player and improviser, Chauvin might have been as great a composer of ragtime as Joplin himself, but he lacked the ambition, discipline, and temperament. While Joplin studiously avoided the excessive pleasures of the district, Chauvin gave in to them with an enthusiasm that could only be called selfdestructive.

By the time Joplin caught up with him in Chicago, Chauvin was a shell of his former self. He was hopelessly addicted to opium and his body was ravaged by syphilis and multiple sclerosis. Joplin was shocked at the sight of his friend and vowed to help him in any way he could. Unable to play professionally any longer, Chauvin had tried to compose but disease and the opium made it impossible for him to concentrate long enough to finish a rag. Joplin looked over the fragments of music scattered on scraps of paper throughout Chauvin's dingy room and found two exquisitely beautiful themes. He worked on the harmonies, added two themes of his own, and fashioned them into a rag. The result was the "Heliotrope Bouquet," published by John Stark in 1907, one of ragtime's most hauntingly beautiful works and Joplin's finest collaboration. Joplin hoped the profits from the rag would help Chauvin get back on his feet and compose more music. But it came too late. The doomed musician died only a few months after the publication of the only rag to bear his name. Chauvin was twenty-seven. Thanks to Scott Joplin, his uniquely sensuous music has been preserved for posterity.

Chauvin's tragic early end must have had its effect on Joplin. Unable to find much work as a musician in Chicago and still too despondent to compose on his own without a collaborator, Joplin said good-bye to the Marshalls and moved on. It was the last time the two friends would see each other.

Like many people who have lost their way in life, Joplin turned to the past for refuge and guidance. He went home to Texarkana. He hadn't been in touch with his family for nine long years and was anxious to see how they were doing. He was saddened by the death of his mother, who had started him on his musical career. But his father was still alive and living with his brother Monroe and his family at 815 Ash Street. His brother Ossie and sister Myrtle had married and moved away, but his other sisters were still in town and were overjoyed to see him. Joplin was cheered at the local music store, where he played his rags. He taught his niece Netty the "Maple Leaf Rag," and he even paid a visit to his old music teacher, J.C. Johnson, who had fallen on hard times. Joplin gave him some money to help him out. The composer stayed only a few days in Texarkana and would never return home again.

Where he went next is uncertain. He probably spent some time back in St. Louis with Tom Turpin and his family and may even have traveled to Germany and other parts of Europe with his mentor Alfred Ernst. If Joplin did make this ambitious journey, there is unfortunately no record of his impressions of Europe. Europe, however, was as mad about ragtime as America. Bold, modern composers like France's Claude Debussy and Russia's Igor Stravinsky even incorporated elements of ragtime, however inaccurately, into their classical compositions.

Wherever Joplin traveled, the change of scenery must have helped him get over his depression, for by 1907 he was once again writing and publishing on a regular basis. His new rags, however, were markedly different from the earlier ones. They were more personal, lyrical and had a new depth of feeling. Belle died about a year after their separation and this event, plus the earlier death of his daughter, brought shadows into the sunlight of his music. As Rudi Blesh has noted, "These melodies and their harmonizations became the pages of the secret diary of an intensely private and searching nature."[2]

Drawing of Scott Joplin

The turning point in the lifting of Joplin's depression was a trip to New York City sometime in 1907 to visit his publisher John Stark. Stark had opened a New York office of his ever-expanding publishing firm in 1905, while keeping his main headquarters back in St. Louis. It was a wise move, for by this time New York was the nation's music publishing capital.

But the ragtime music that came out of New York bore little resemblance to the classic, graceful compositions of Joplin, Marshall, Hayden, and other composers from the Midwest. New York ragtime was fast, raucous, and brashly commercial, like the city itself. This music was far easier for the average amateur to master, and by 1907 it was far more popular than classic piano rags. It also lent itself to songs that could be sung and had a wider appeal than did simple piano pieces. In fact, many of the so-called rags that came out of the eastern cities were not rags at all but pop songs that used rag rhythms and incorporated "rag" or "ragtime" in their titles. Perhaps the best known of these songs is "Alexander's Ragtime Band" (1911), by a Russian immigrant named Israel Baline who had changed his name to Irving Berlin. Although it had a ragtime hook, Berlin's popular song was no more a true piano rag than his later hit "White Christmas."

Berlin and other ambitious young songwriters toiled at their pianos in a neighborhood of downtown Manhattan that was so noisy from their music making that the neighbors came to call it "Tin Pan Alley." It was a name by which an entire new era in American pop music would be known.

Joplin's reign as "king of ragtime" was coming to an end, at least in the East. His rags were being pushed out of the spotlight by the compositions of many lesser but more commercially minded composers. "Aside from the 'Maple Leaf Rag' there were few [Joplin rags] that attained popularity," recalled ragtime pianist W. N. H. Harding in 1964. "I played his 'Pine-Apple,' 'Cascades,' and a few others, but for the most part, it was the rags of Wenrich, Bernard, Snyder, and similar composers that were used, and all our local boys had special numbers of their own."[3]

There was, however, at least one young white composer in New York who thought Scott Joplin was still the king of ragtime. Joseph Lamb was born in Montclair, New Jersey, in 1887. He started out studying to be an engineer at the Stevens Institute of Technology in Hoboken, New Jersey, but was soon writing songs and waltzes, some of which were published in Canada while he was still a student. In 1907 Lamb discovered classic ragtime and was immediately infatuated with it. He wrote several rags of his own in the Joplin style and submitted them to John Stark at his New York music store. Stark rejected Lamb's work, but Lamb wasn't discouraged by Stark's rejection and continued to hang around the music store, hoping for a change of heart.

One day later that same year he accidentally met his idol. It was a meeting that would change his life. Here, years later, is how Lamb described it:

> There was a colored fellow sitting there with his foot bandaged up as if he had the gout, and a crutch beside him. I told Mrs. Stark that I liked the Joplin rags best and wanted to get any I didn't have. The colored fellow spoke up and asked whether I had certain pieces which he named. I thanked him and bought several and was leaving when I said to Mrs. Stark that Joplin was one fellow I would certainly like to meet. "Really," said Mrs. Stark, "Well, here's your man." I shook hands with him, needless to say. It was a thrill I've never forgotten. I had met Scott Joplin and was going home to tell the folks.[4]

Joplin took an interest in the enthusiastic young composer and invited him over to the house where he was staying to play his rags for him and some friends. When Joplin heard Lamb's "Sensation Rag," he called it "a regular Negro rag."[5] He could not have paid Lamb a higher compliment. Joplin generously offered to resubmit the rag to Stark and even agreed to add his name on the first page as arranger. He knew that would help win over Stark and promote sales for the unknown composer. It is possible Joplin was doing for Lamb what the white composer Charles Daniels did for him when he helped Joplin's first rag, "Original Rags," get published.

Later Stark called Lamb and told him he'd pay him twenty-five dollars for his "Sensation Rag" and another twenty-five when one thousand copies were sold. "He could have had it for nothing,"[6] Lamb later commented. Lamb's career as a ragtime composer was launched and his rags continued to be published by Stark and Son until 1919. Today Joseph Lamb's name stands alongside Scott Joplin and James Scott as one of the "big three" of ragtime's golden era.

The year 1907 was a good one for composer Scott Joplin as well. He published five rags, including "Heliotrope Bouquet" and "Gladiolus Rag," his best rag since "The Cascades" three years earlier. Similar in style to "Maple Leaf Rag," "Gladiolus Rag" is a well-constructed composition with strong development that showed a new maturity in Joplin's composing. "Searchlight Rag" was written in honor of his friend Tom Turpin, who prospected for gold in the town of Searchlight, Nevada, years earlier. The influence of Turpin's lively playing style is evident in this rollicking rag. "Lily Queen" was Joplin's second collaboration with Arthur Marshall, written when he stayed with his friend in Chicago. Marshall later claimed that the composition was his exclusively.

"Joplin told me he had a party that would publish that piece of music, so I let him handle it," Marshall wrote with undisguised bitterness in a letter. "But for him having any part in the composing, he did not. Now he was the more popular as a composer and that is why his name was mentioned in the writing. . . . I got about fifty dollars in all for it at the time. . . ."

It seems out of character for Joplin to take credit where it wasn't due, and if he did allow his name to be used, it might have been to help his friend get published.

New York, besides being the center of music publishing, was the center of American theater. Broadway was lined with theaters, the most popular of which featured a form of live entertainment known as vaudeville. The word "vaudeville" is French and referred to a light play with music popular during the nineteenth century. But in the United States, vaudeville came to mean quite a different kind of theatrical fare. The form originated not, as minstrel shows did, in legitimate theaters, but in the kind of saloons and honky-tonks in which Scott Joplin played ragtime. Owners of saloons reasoned that if a pianist drew more customers to their establishment, then more musicians and singers would only increase their business. So the larger establishments put up crude stages and hired singers, dancers, and larger musical ensembles to perform for patrons on a regular schedule during the day and evening.

These shows were at first called "variety" because they contained a wide range of acts. By the 1890s, these variety shows were taking on a life of their own and moved out of the disreputable saloons into legitimate theaters, where they became respectable entertainment. Tony Pastor, the king of vaudeville producers, made vaudeville even more respectable by banning alcohol from his theaters and adding more family-oriented fare, such as magicians, comedians, jugglers, and animal acts. Pastor's Opera House in New York City became the showcase for the top performers of the day, many of whom would go on later to even greater careers in radio, movies, and television. Vaudeville would remain one of the most popular forms of entertainment in the United States—until the early 1930s, when it was killed off by radio and sound movies.

Vaudeville held an enticing appeal for Scott Joplin,

A typical vaudeville skit

Broadway at West Forty-third street, New York City, in 1909, when the Joplins lived at 252 West Forty-seventh street

who saw it as a chance to cash in on his public image and make enough money to return full time to composing. Among the eight to ten acts on a vaudeville bill in a large theater like Tony Pastor's Opera House, Joplin would surely have been a headliner. He was grandly billed as "King of Ragtime Composers—Author of `Maple Leaf Rag.'" As he did in his previous career as a performer, Joplin traveled from city to city on the vaudeville circuit, living out of boardinghouses and cheap hotels.

Little is known of Joplin's experiences on the vaudeville circuit, but he must have enjoyed performing his work in a legitimate theater and having the appreciative attention of a paying audience, even if he were preceded by a magician or a family of barking dogs.

While performing in Washington, D.C., Joplin met Lottie Stokes, a young black woman who loved his music and was attracted to the man who created it. In Lottie, Scott found the woman he longed for—someone who appreciated his talents and would support and encourage him in all his creative endeavors. They were engaged and married probably in 1909. They traveled together on the vaudeville circuit for a while and then settled in New York, where Lottie turned Scott's home there, at 252 West Forty-seventh Street, into a boardinghouse for young musicians. Joplin started teaching again and set up a studio and his own publishing house.

During this happy and fruitful time, Joplin envisioned a new work that would incorporate everything he had learned and done up until then. It would be an ambitious creation that would pick up where he left off in his experimental attempts to merge classical musical forms with ragtime and other popular black music. This new work would be an opera, a far more sophisticated one than *A Guest of Honor*. It would be a full-length work in the grand opera tradition and include not only ragtime but every kind of music on the American musical scene. It would be, Joplin was convinced, his crowning achievement, his true masterpiece.

TREEMONISHA

Music circles have been stirred recently by the announcement that Scott Joplin, known as the apostle of ragtime, is composing scores for grand opera.[1]

—*New York Age, March 5, 1908*

Since the mid-1960s, it sometimes seems that our distinctions between "high" art and "popular" art, particularly in the world of music, have all but vanished. In those years, such cultural leaders as composer and conductor Leonard Bernstein praised the music of such pop groups as the Beatles, comparing a ballad by Lennon and McCartney to the art songs of nineteenth-century German composer Franz Schubert. Of course, Bernstein himself had helped blur the line between classical and popular music by writing a string of successful Broadway musicals, most notably *West Side Story* (1957), a modern reworking of Shakespeare's *Romeo and Juliet.*

Then in 1967, the first rock musical, *Hair,* brought rock and roll and other pop-music styles to the Broadway stage, and became the hit of the theatrical season. Peter Townshend of the British rock group The Who took things a step further with his rock opera, *Tommy* (1969). *Tommy* eventually made it to Broadway in 1992 and won the Tony Award for best score and best musical. Today, for any pop composer to write in a classical form, such as opera, is acceptable and often lauded. But it was not that way in Scott Joplin's day.

In the early years of the twentieth century, the idea of mixing classical forms with popular music was inconceivable. The world of the concert hall and the world of entertainment were strictly segregated and never the twain could meet. The American musical establishment was snobbish in its tastes and thoroughly conservative. Probably this was mostly due to its own cultural insecurity. America, although a major world power by 1910, was culturally still in the shadow of Europe and its thousand-year-old heritage. It was all right for American composers Edward MacDowell and Louis Gottschalk to use local material such as Native American and Creole themes in their music, but the music had to conform to European classical forms—the sonata, the concerto, the symphony. The Negro rag, although a blend of American and European music, did not qualify as such a form and was viewed by most cultural critics as commercial trash. So when Scott Joplin began working on a grand opera that would incorporate nearly every kind of popular music of the day, he must have known he was looking for trouble.

The date Joplin first conceived his second opera is uncertain. Joseph Lamb claims Joplin played him selections from the score in 1908 and Eubie Blake, another ragtime composer who turned to the stage, has said Joplin told him about it as early as 1907. It is possible Joplin had the idea as early as 1905 and completed a first draft by 1908. By the time he settled in New York with Lottie, he probably had completed a second draft.

The work Joplin called his magnum opus was entitled *Treemonisha*. The unusual title was taken from the name of the central character, an eighteen-year-old black girl. Joplin set his opera, as he wrote in the preface to the libretto, "on a plantation somewhere in the State of Arkansas, northeast of the town of Texarkana and three or four miles from the Red River....The year 1866 finds them [the Negroes on the plantation] in dense ignorance, with no-one to guide them, as the white folks had moved away shortly after the Negroes were set free and had left the plantation in charge of a trustworthy Negro servant named Ned."[2]

Ned and his wife Monisha are childless and pray for a baby of their own to raise. Their prayers are answered one night when Monisha finds a light-brown-skinned baby girl under a tree in front of their cabin. The couple raise the girl as their own and when she turns seven they ask a neighboring white woman to educate her. Thus the girl becomes the only educated black person on the plantation. Later, in her solo, "Treemonisha's Bringing Up," Monisha explains how she came to name her:

> Monisha first I named you,
> The honor was for me,
> Treemonisha next I named you,
> Because you loved that tree.[3]

The action of the opera starts in 1884, when Treemonisha is eighteen. The plantation people are kept in ignorance by a band of conjurers, or magicians, who practice witchcraft. They are led by Zodzetrik, Luddud, and Simon, three old men who earn their living by selling little luck-bags and rabbits' feet to the residents. Treemonisha gently rebukes the conjurors and tells them to end their witchery and free the people from their superstitions. Angered by her rebuke and fearing her power, Zodzetrik and Luddud kidnap Treemonisha while she is out with a friend gathering leaves for a wreath. They take her to the conjurors' meeting in the forest and prepare to throw her into a wasp's nest to punish her for defying them. She is saved by her friend Remus, disguised as a scarecrow. The conjurors believe Remus is the devil and flee for their lives. Treemonisha returns safely home to her parents. Zodzetrik and Luddud are captured by a group of the plantation blacks and brought before Treemonisha. She pleads for their release, saying forgiveness is more important than revenge.

When Treemonisha tells the people they need a leader to take them out of their ignorance and help them improve their lives, they immediately ask her to be that leader. She accepts the position and ends the opera by leading the company in a rag dance of celebration.

The central message of *Treemonisha* is as straightforward and simple as its story—education is the pathway to freedom and progress for black Americans. It was a message delivered previously by other important African-Americans, from Frederick Douglass to Booker T. Washington, but never before had the point been made so profoundly by a black creative artist.

Far more controversial in its day was Joplin's pointed feminism. In the sublime choral number "We Will Trust You As Our Leader," Treemonisha herself is unsure her people will accept a woman, and a young one at that, as their leader and guide.

TREEMONISHA
Women may follow me many days long,
But the men may think that I am wrong.

MEN
No, no, no, no!

CHORUS (all)
We all agree to trust you,
And we will be true.
We all agree to trust you,
And we will be true.[4]

Despite its revolutionary message, *Treemonisha* is, for a musical drama, curiously lacking in drama. The conflict between Treemonisha and the conjurors takes up little stage time, her capture takes place offstage, and her rescue has all the buffoonery of a vaudeville comedy sketch. The conjurors are stock comic villains with little individuality, and the libretto, by Joplin, who was never a very adept lyricist, is often stilted, cumbersome, and simplistic. Here is a good example from Remus's lecture to the people in Act 3:

> Wrong is never right,
> That is very true,
>
> Wrong is never right,
> And wrong you should not do.
>
> Wrong is never right,
> You will agree with me,
> Wrong is never right,
> And it will never be.[5]

Yet the listener looking for a musical drama on the level of such great opera composers as Richard Wagner or Giuseppe Verdi is missing the point. *Treemonisha* is a folk opera that is more celebratory and ritualistic than dramatic, in the manner of such Shakespearean comedies as *A Midsummer's Night Dream*. Its fairy tale forest is not unlike Shakespeare's in that play nor so different from the magical world of Mozart's opera *The Magic Flute*. "Both works [*The Magic Flute* and *Treemonisha*] can be categorized as spiritual vaudevilles whose pranks shine with a special incandescence. . . ," writes Frank Corsaro, who directed *Treemonisha* in 1975. "Taken literally, the events appear to be so humdrum that they would hardly fill the scope of a one-acter. Seen symbolically—ritualistically—all is inevitable and satisfying."[6]

What is most satisfying about *Treemonisha* is its wonderful music. Unlike *A Guest of Honor*, *Treemonisha* is not a ragtime opera but a work that incorporates every kind

Treemonisha, *Scott Joplin's opera, was performed by the Houston Grand Opera Company in 1982.*

of American popular music that Joplin knew and loved. Out of the twenty-seven separate musical numbers in the show, only three can be called authentic ragtime—the exuberant cornhuskers' dance, "We're Goin' Around"; the rollicking "Dinah Has Blowed De Horn," which closes the second act; and the climactic "A Real Slow Drag." The other numbers employ the musical styles of Negro spirituals, church hymns, popular ballads, barbershop quartet, choral music, and the more traditional European operatic arias, or solo numbers, and recitatives, speechlike singing that moves the story forward.

Despite its distinctly American music, *Treemonisha* follows the form of a European opera. It has a full overture before the story begins and instrumental preludes that open the first and third acts. There is even a ballet of sorts in the second act, the humorous "Frolic of the Bears," in which eight bears drop by for a dance in the forest before Treemonisha's rescue.

What makes *Treemonisha* work for a modern, sophisticated audience is the heartfelt sincerity of its creator. Although there is a certain artificiality to a few of the musical numbers—such as Remus's "Wrong Is Never Right," with its straining to sound like an operatic aria—most of the music sounds incredibly fresh and natural, in spite of the European conventions that have been imposed on it. A simple line like "Does you feel lak you've been redeemed?"—addressed by Parson Alltalk to his congregation—is lifted to a level of pure spirituality by Joplin's hymnlike music. Similarly, Monisha's big aria, "The Sacred Tree," skillfully uses the sentimental ballad form to create one of the opera's most moving moments, as the mother tells her daughter and the community about her origins.

Perhaps Joplin wrote with such conviction because the story of *Treemonisha* is very much his own story. The autobiographical parallels are obvious. The setting is near his own hometown, and the dilemma facing Monisha and Ned is one that was faced by the composer's own parents trying to make their way in the world in the wake of slavery. Like Monisha, Joplin's own mother put him on the path to his career, by getting him access to the pianos in the white homes in which she worked. Like Monisha, she even found him a white teacher to educate him, J. C. Johnson.

If the story is a metaphor for black independence and self-sufficiency following the end of slavery, it can also be seen as the story of black music itself—a music that gave Joplin and many other blacks the opportunity to rise above the station of manual laborer to become creative artists. In his opera, Joplin attempted to raise that music from the saloon to the temple of high culture, showing it to be an integral part of American life and worthy of the same degree of respect given the classical music of Europe.

The point is made no more powerfully than in the opera's final number, "A Real Slow Drag." This is no mere social dance Treemonisha leads her people in but a grand anthem of their cultural heritage. What begins in Treemonisha's solo as a melancholy rag builds up in full chorus to a majestic march from a dark, painful past into a bright and joyful future.

> *Marching onward, marching onward,*
> *Marching to that lovely tune;*
> *Marching onward, marching onward,*
> *Happy as a bird in June.*[7]

For all its oddities, eccentricities, and faults, *Treemonisha* is a true American original, a bold work infused with deep feeling, proclaiming a message of black liberation that is just as applicable today as it was in Joplin's time.

Joplin labored at his opera for at least two years. By 1910, he felt ready to show it to his friend and publisher John Stark. Today, a composer or dramatist might get his work produced and worry about publishing it later. In this time before tapes, CDs, and original cast recordings, sheet music was the main way a composer made money

In the Houston Grand Opera's production of Treemonisha, *the title role was played by Carmen Balthrop.*

on his or her property. Joplin might well have known what Stark's reaction would be, but he had such tremendous faith in his opera that even this fear didn't stop him. Stark had already indulged Joplin by publishing his folk ballet and said he wouldn't consider publishing a work twenty times that length. To give Stark his due, Joplin had come to him with his opera at a bad time. Tin Pan Alley's pop music had seriously hurt the sales of Stark and Joplin's classic rags and business was miserable. Then in 1910, Stark's wife, who had been seriously ill for some time, died. Depressed and in financial straits, Stark decided to close his New York operation and return to his home base in St. Louis.

But before he left New York Stark asked Joplin to waive his royalty rights and accept a flat, one-time fee on all future compositions. Joplin was understandably upset, feeling he had been betrayed by the one man in music publishing he had come to trust. Stark, in his turn, felt Joplin was making unfair demands on him in a difficult time when his business was in serious trouble. If Joplin could say no to him, he could do the same. He refused to publish any more of Joplin's music. Thus, in one angry moment, the longest and most famous relationship in American music publishing to that time came to an end. John Stark returned to St. Louis to salvage what remained of his publishing business, while Scott Joplin started looking for a new publisher for his grand opera.

Although *Treemonisha* would increasingly dominate Joplin's creative energies, he still found time to write rags. In 1908 he wrote a trio of "fruit" rags—"Fig Leaf Rag," "Sugar Cane," and "Pine-Apple Rag." The first of these was his last solo effort published by Stark (except for the posthumous "Reflection Rag" of 1917). Nearly all of Joplin's remaining compositions, except for his opera, would be published by the New York firm of Seminary Music.

"Fig Leaf Rag," subtitled "a high-class rag," began a period of intense experimentation that would continue until the appearance of his last rag, in 1914. In these rags Joplin pushed the form he had helped create to its limits. One of the constants of ragtime was the steady rhythmic beat played by the left hand, which gave the music its distinctive sound. But it also made the ragtime composer a prisoner of its "oom-pah" beat. Joplin began to "free up" the left hand, making it more independent—even letting it carry the melody at times. The later rags are also characterized—as Guy Waterman points out in his 1956 article "Joplin's Late Rags: An Analysis," by complex harmonies, longer phrasing, extensive modulations, greater structural balance, and a more muted syncopation.

How far Joplin had come from the early, sunny days of "Maple Leaf Rag" can be seen most strikingly in his first published rag of 1909, the "Wall Street Rag." The title is significant and shows the impact living in New York had on the composer. For the first and only time, Joplin wrote a descriptive heading to each of the rag's four sections that illustrates in a little story the power of music to overcome human ills, even those of a cold-hearted Wall Street broker:

1. Panic in Wall Street, Brokers feeling melancholy; 2. Good times coming; 3. Good times have come; 4. Listening to the strains of genuine Negro ragtime, Brokers forget their cares.[8]

The music follows this programmatic outline in ways that take Joplin into uncharted musical territory. The first strain is an intricate, twisting melancholy theme that captivates the ear. In the second strain the melancholy mood lessens but is still prominent. The third strain, according to Peter Gammond, "has a distinctly vaudeville air about it and suggests the theatrical potential of Joplin's future work."[9] The fourth strain bursts into the sunlight, banishing all shadows with spiraling notes that end this gorgeous rag in a cheerful climax.

86

"Wall Street Rag" was followed the same year by "Solace," a beautiful "Mexican serenade," Joplin's only composition set to a tango rhythm; "Pleasant Moments," a ragtime waltz less memorable than "Bethena"; "Euphonic Sounds," even more experimental and intricate than "Wall Street Rag"; and "Paragon Rag," which recaptures some of the simplicity and brightness of his earlier rags.

As Joplin was reaching his creative peak as a ragtime composer, the public was turning away from classic rag in favor of Tin Pan Alley's pallid but tuneful imitations of ragtime. What troubled Joplin even more than this watered-down ragtime was the effect it had on the way his own compositions were played by both professional and amateur musicians. "Notice! Don't play this piece fast," Joplin had written on the sheet music for his 1905 rag "Leola." "It is never right to play 'rag-time' fast."[10]

For Joplin, playing his music at a fast, breakneck pace robbed it of all its grace, subtlety, and fragile beauty. He felt so strongly about this that in 1908 he wrote a brief instructional manual, *School of Ragtime*, which he published himself. The manual contained six exercises of increasing difficulty for the amateur player that, in the composer's words, would "assist players in giving the 'Joplin Rags' that weird and intoxicating effect intended by the composer." More important, the *School of Ragtime* contains the composer's only extensive writing about his music that we have. Here is an excerpt:

> *What is scurrilously called ragtime is an invention that is here to stay. That is now conceded by all classes of musicians. That all publications masquerading under the name of ragtime are not the genuine article will be better known when these exercises are studied. That real ragtime of the higher class is rather difficult to play is a painful truth which most pianists have discovered. Syncopations are no indication of light or trashy*

music, and to shy bricks at "hateful ragtime" no longer passes for musical culture.[11]

Although he exudes confidence in this preface, Joplin privately confided to Joseph Lamb that he doubted *School of Ragtime* would change the direction in which more commercial ragtime was headed. Nevertheless, his own rags and those of Stark's other classic-rag composers continued to sell modestly well outside the large northern cities, particularly in the South.

But for the one work he most wanted to present to the musical public, Joplin was unable to find a publisher. He toiled up and down Tin Pan Alley, playing selections from *Treemonisha* for one music publisher after another. None wanted to risk publishing his opera, even those few who found it interesting.

Discouraged but hardly defeated, Joplin made a fateful decision. He had published his own music before and he could do it again. The challenge was a daunting one. A rag took up only a few pages of sheet music, while a three-act opera would require reams of paper and be very expensive. The composer had to write only the piano part for his rags, and, in the case of a song, one vocal line. *Treemonisha* would require parts for eleven voices and a chorus as well as the piano accompaniment. It was a gargantuan task that would take nearly all Joplin's energies for a year. Little time or energy would be left for writing other music.

In 1910, Joplin published only two pieces—a song version of "Pine-Apple Rag," with uninspired lyrics by Joe Snyder, and the charming, wonderfully innovative "Stoptime Rag." This uniquely syncopated rag included these instructions from the composer:

To get the desired effect of "Stoptime" the pianist should stomp the heel of one foot upon the floor, wherever the word "stamp" appears in the music.[12]

Tin Pan Alley, where Scott Joplin tried desperately to have the music of his opera published

The score of *Treemonisha*, all 270 pages of it, finally appeared in 1911. Sales were almost nil, but at least one music critic recognized the genius of its composer. "[He] has created an original type of music in which he employs syncopation in a most artistic and original manner," wrote a critic in the June 1911 issue of *American Musician*. "Moreover, he has created an entirely new phase of musical art and has produced a thoroughly American opera."[13]

These words must have given Joplin new hope after so much rejection. Here was a member of the musical establishment who recognized and appreciated what he had tried to accomplish and believed he had succeeded. Soon the entire nation would know as well, but for that to happen Joplin would have to take the next step—he would have to bring *Treemonisha* to life, not on the printed page, but on the dramatic stage.

CRUSHED DREAMS

Without scenery, costumes, lighting or orchestral backing, the drama seemed thin and unconvincing, little better than a rehearsal. . . .[1]

—Sam Patterson, friend and orchestrator of Treemonisha

When Scott Joplin began working on his great opera, it was a passion; by the time he had published the vocal-piano score in 1911, it had become an obsession. Getting *Treemonisha* produced dominated his every waking moment. The creative drive in this gifted composer's life turned in on itself and became a force for self-destruction. Joplin all but stopped working on any other compositions; he would produce only four more rags in his lifetime, two of these collaborations with Scott Hayden. He would begin to alienate his students and, after a time, stop taking on new ones. Activities in the happy Joplin household, always a warm gathering place for musicians and composers, took a sinister turn. To keep the money coming in after the loss of students, Lottie Joplin transformed their home into a discreet brothel.

The finale of Treemonisha

The nervousness, anxiety, and erratic behavior that became more and more a part of Joplin's personality did not all stem from *Treemonisha*. By 1911, as all the evidence now points, Scott Joplin was a very sick man. Although he had escaped the degradation that befell Louis Chauvin and others, the sins of the district finally caught up with him. At some time during his wandering years, Joplin contracted the venereal disease syphilis. Although hardly a profligate, Joplin had affairs with at least several women during the breakup of his marriage. His womanizing may even have contributed to his separation from Belle, although there is little hard evidence. We do know that a number of Joplin's rags were dedicated to other women— Minnie L. Montgomery, Miss Minnie Wade, and Marie Antoinette Willis, who also may have inspired the title of his 1906 march.

Today, syphilis can be cured with a shot of penicillin. In Joplin's days it was a death sentence, a kind of slow-working multiple sclerosis for which there was as yet no real cure. From the description of him by his contemporaries, the disease was already advanced enough to have affected his nervous system by the time he had settled in New York with Lottie. "He could hardly talk," recalled Eubie Blake, who met Joplin briefly around 1908. "He was sick—his health was gone, he was very ill. . . [later] he went to the piano and played. It was pitiful. I almost cried. . . ."[2]

Knowing perhaps that time was running out, Joplin worked desperately to get his masterpiece produced. For two solid years he hounded dozens of producers, showing them the glowing review of his score from the *American Musician* and playing selections from his opera. All to no avail. No one wanted to gamble on such an obviously noncommercial work, not when there were plenty of more appealing comedies and musicals to fill the New York theaters.

In 1913, however, it looked as if all of Joplin's efforts might pay off. Benjamin Nibur, manager of the Lafayette

Theater in Harlem, expressed interest in putting on *Treemonisha*. Months passed, and Nibur kept putting the composer off about a production date. Finally, he contacted Joplin and told him the theater would be ready for his opera in the fall. Joplin was stunned. It was already August. How could he possibly put together a full production of the opera with its many facets in only a month or two? The composer immediately put a casting call and announcement for the show in the *New York Age*. That was the last ever heard of the production. The Lafayette Theater came under new management and all plans for *Treemonisha* were dropped. It was a heavy blow to Joplin, who went into a deep depression.

Despite depression and failing health, Joplin managed to write several rags in these years, when *Treemonisha* overshadowed everything else in his life. These remarkable compositions carried his experimentation with the piano rag form to its furthest degree.

"Scott Joplin's New Rag" (1912) is something of a misnomer. It partly looks back to the past and his earlier rhythmic, happy style. But at the same time the rag looks forward to the future with its astonishing combination of sunlight and shadows. The opening theme, while jaunty, is nervous and anxious. It is riddled with a mounting sense of frustration that not only captures Joplin's frame of mind at the time but expresses a profound fatalism in the face of life's troubles. The second strain deepens the melancholy, as does the last strain, which is surprisingly brief and transitory in nature. The first theme is repeated not twice but three times, to drive home the point.

"Magnetic Rag" (1914) has been called by David Jasen and Terbor Tichenor "his most intense and personal ragtime essay . . . probably his last rag, certainly his most affecting." "Magnetic Rag" looks fearlessly to the future. It is in every way a breakthrough, taking ragtime into a new realm of popular music that Peter Gammond calls "Chopinesque"[3] in its expression. The first section is deceptively simple, ending in a syncopated stomping beat that is more desperate than joyful. The second strain, also in a minor key, is sad and reflective. The third strain comes the closest to old-time ragtime, but its stomping is more complex and twisty than the early rags. The fourth strain is less a theme than a moody transitional section, that leads us back to the original theme with strong effect. The coda that rounds off this singularly memorable rag is quiet, gentle and sadly beautiful. With "Magnetic Rag" Scott Joplin pointed the way to a new kind of music that was so personal and intimate, so expressive of every emotion, that it is akin to a Chopin étude or a Beethoven sonata. Sadly, the genre went no further. It was to be Joplin's last rag.

In 1913 he published two musical numbers from *Treemonisha*—"A Real Slow Drag" and the "Prelude to Act 3." In 1915, "The Frolic of the Bears," one of the dance sequences from his opera, would appear. These generated little interest in the larger work and little income as well. Joplin needed money—badly.

After the disappointment of the aborted Lafayette Theater engagement, Joplin decided that the only way he could interest a producer in his work was to produce a fully orchestrated score. To help him in this colossal undertaking, he enlisted an old friend and ragtime musician from St. Louis, Sam Patterson. To pay Patterson and cover his own living expenses, Scott and Lottie moved out of the big house on West Forty-seventh Street and rented a smaller house in Harlem at 163 West 131st Street. The two men worked ceaselessly night and day for two months in Joplin's basement. As Joplin would finish a part in the orchestral master score, Patterson would immediately begin copying it.

According to Patterson, they would stop work at noon, when Lottie would serve them lunch. "Joplin said, 'Let's knock off, I hear Lottie coming,'" recalled Patterson. "Just then the phone rang and I went to answer it. When I came back, there were fried eggs on the table and Lottie was opening a bottle of champagne some folks she worked for had given her. I said, 'These eggs are cold,' and Scott said, 'Look Sam, if they're good hot, they're good cold.'"⁴

When the orchestrations were finished and still no producer came forward to stage the work, Joplin made a fateful decision. He would stage it himself. And why not? He had done the same with his first opera and *The Ragtime Dance*, and the results had been professional. Of course, given his financial straits, he could never afford to stage a full production of the opera with scenery, costumes, and an orchestra in the pit. Instead, he would put on a kind of dress rehearsal. Even without all these production values, Joplin firmly believed that the producers he would invite to this single performance would see the merits of his opera and provide the financing for a full production. To help convince these money people, he would invite the general public—both black and white theatergoers—and trust that their enthusiastic reception of his work would further convince producers it was worth backing.

Joplin rented the Lincoln Theatre at 135th Street in Harlem and went about casting and rehearsing his opera. Since there was no money to hire an orchestra, Joplin provided the only musical accompaniment, on the piano, himself. Because he couldn't afford to pay the singers and dancers much, he couldn't ask them to put in many rehearsals. As a result, they were woefully underrehearsed as the evening of the performance drew near.

In certain movies the outcome of such an endeavor is always preordained. The long-suffering composer and his loyal cast and crew rent a hall and put on their original show. The audience is captivated by the performance and leaves the theater humming the show's tunes. Producers rush backstage to congratulate the composer and offer to put the show on Broadway, where it is, of course, the hit of the season. The composer and his wife get rich from the show's royalties and live happily ever after.

It's a familiar scenario, but real life is far less certain. On that night in 1915 there was no standing ovation for

*Harlem, where Scott Joplin produced his
opera himself in 1915*

Scott Joplin in the Lincoln Theater. The small audience of mostly friends sat in stony silence when the curtain came down. If there was any applause it was tepid at best. People were bewildered and disappointed. There was none of the spectacle and opulence they had come to expect from opera—just a group of singers and dancers in street clothes on a bare stage performing to the sound of a piano. One of the few people present that night who recorded their impressions was the loyal Sam Patterson, and even he could not be encouraging. "Without scenery, costumes, lighting, or orchestral backing, the drama seemed thin and unconvincing, little better than a rehearsal, and its special quality, in any event, would surely have been lost on the typical Harlem audience that attended."[5]

That Harlem audience was probably offended and embarrassed by what it saw on stage. By 1915, some blacks had begun to make great strides economically and socially in the United States, particularly in the North. There was a small but growing black middle class in many northern cities, including New York, and undoubtedly a good part of the blacks who came to see *Treemonisha* were from this group. They saw the opera's southern plantation setting and the simple, naive choruses of cornhuskers and cotton pickers as a part of their past they would rather forget. Joplin's music, with its plantation dances, folksongs, simple hymns, and touches of ragtime, were also negative reminders of slavery and southern roots these more sophisticated city dwellers didn't want to return to. Joplin's message of liberation through education and the advancement of women was all but lost on these people, who couldn't see past the opera's other elements.

Treemonisha might have been better appreciated by an audience that could look on the work with less personal involvement. But because the theater was in Harlem and featured an all-black cast, few white operagoers were willing to venture uptown to see it. It would be another five years or more before whites flocked to the theaters of Harlem to see blacks perform, sing, and dance during the so-called Harlem Renaissance of the 1920s.

In one sense Joplin and his opera were too early; in another sense, they were too late. Plays and musicals that dealt with black life had made their way to Broadway by 1898 with black composer Will Marion Cook's *Clorindy, or the Origin of the Cakewalk*. A later Cook hit, *In Dahomey*, even used ragtime and European musical forms, although it was not an opera. Unfortunately for Joplin, the vogue for black shows died out five years before his ill-fated performance of *Treemonisha*.

What was popular in 1915 were shows that set the stage for the emergence of the American Broadway musical as we know it today. These were the smart, snappy revues of Irving Berlin and the first book musicals of Jerome Kern at the famed Princess Theater. Twelve years later, Kern, with lyricist Oscar Hammerstein II, would create the first truly dramatic musical—*Showboat*. It would contain black characters and a good imitation of black folk music ("Ol' Man River") and a story that was as full of Americana as *Treemonisha*. Seven years later, in 1935, twenty years after *Treemonisha*'s premiere, a white American composer, George Gershwin, was hailed for daring to put popular music into an opera about simple black folk in Charleston, South Carolina. *Porgy and Bess* would become the most popular American opera of the twentieth century. But Scott Joplin and *Treemonisha* had been there first.

FINAL CURTAIN

Scott Joplin is dead. A homeless itinerant, he left his mark on American music.[1]

—John Stark

The failure of *Treemonisha* was a crushing blow to Scott Joplin, one from which he never recovered. For years the dream of his masterwork's success sustained him through heartbreak, failing health, and disappointments. He believed it would complete the bridge between popular and classical music that he had begun to build ten years earlier with *The Ragtime Dance*. Now the bridge and the dream collapsed before his eyes and all hope was lost.

Perhaps what was most terrible about the reception of *Treemonisha* was not the failure of his own people—the blacks of Harlem—to understand what he was doing, but the complete silence from the musical establishment. The same critics who vehemently attacked his rags as poisonous "ragweed,"[2] had nothing to say either for or against his folk opera. For many, the very idea of a black man writing an opera with popular music was ludicrous and beneath the dignity of criticism. If they had ranted and railed against *Treemonisha*, Joplin might have fought onward, but being ignored was more than he could bear.

Following that fateful night, *Treemonisha* disappeared into oblivion. Joplin had no resources to stage another dress rehearsal, and even if he had the financial backing to do so, he didn't have the heart to undertake it. His finest work, the one he had labored on for years, had been rejected by the public and he was devastated.

Another event took place that terrible year of 1915 that must have left its mark on his mental and physical health. Scott Hayden, Joplin's friend, pupil, and collaborator on four rags, died at the age of thirty-three of pulmonary tuberculosis in Chicago's Cook County Hospital. Hayden, whose rags written with Joplin were his only published works, had never been able to make a living with his music. For the last twelve years of his life he had worked as an elevator operator in the same hospital in which he died.

Joplin's illness was both physical and mental. The syphilis attacked his nervous system and affected his mind. He couldn't concentrate on composing, could barely play the piano, and was depressed for long periods. His behavior became more and more erratic after the debacle of his opera. One moment he would be happy and content; the next, angry and frustrated. He became paranoid and began accusing people, even close friends, of trying to steal his music.

When a publisher commissioned Joplin to orchestrate several of his early rags, Lottie hoped that the work would lift his spirits and bring him out of his depression. But he found it impossible to focus for long on the work and left orchestrations of at least two rags, "Searchlight Rag" and "Stoptime Rag," unfinished. The Uni-Record Piano-Roll Company asked him to make new rolls of some rags. Pianolas, or player pianos, were becoming more popular than regular pianos in America and the companies that manufactured them often hired the original composers to make rolls of their work. These rolls, the last record of Scott Joplin the musician, were poorly played and so full of mistakes that Uni-Record had to fix them later. The only roll they left untouched was Joplin's flawed performance of the "Maple Leaf Rag." According to ragtime historian Terry Waldo this roll "provides a sad yet fascinating insight into Joplin's tortured mind a few months before the final breakdown."[3]

When that breakdown occurred, in early 1917, Joplin was a shell of his former self. He couldn't write or play piano and could barely speak. He was losing all physical coordination. Heartbroken, Lottie realized she could no longer take care of her husband and had no choice but to institutionalize him. On March 29, the following item appeared in the New York Age: "Scott Joplin, composer of the "Maple Leaf Rag" and other syncopated melodies, is a patient at Ward's Island for mental trouble."[4] Actually, Joplin had been admitted to the Manhattan State Hospital on tiny Ward's Island in the East River some eight weeks earlier.

At first he fluctuated between periods of lucidity, when he would write down notes furiously on paper, and periods of lassitude, when he would barely react to the life around him. Gradually his lucid periods became more infrequent, and by the time the news item appeared, he no longer recognized the few friends who came to visit him.

He died on April 1, 1917, the same day the United States entered World War I. The death certificate attributed his demise to "dementia paralytica—cerebral" and "syphilis."[5] Lottie felt there were other factors. "You might say he died of disappointment . . . ,"[6] she later said.

The funeral took place five days later. It was attended by his widow and some of his New York friends, including S. Brunson Campbell, the so-called Ragtime Kid, who

Player piano roll is being corrected as
conductor Ernst Schelling watches.

claimed to be Joplin's only white pupil. "Each carriage in his funeral procession carried the name of one of his compositions," Campbell wrote years later. "'Maple Leaf Rag' was on the first."[7] Campbell's description of the funeral as a grand affair has been contradicted by others, who claim the composer was buried in an unmarked pauper's grave.

It was Joplin's last wish that "Maple Leaf Rag" be played at his funeral. Lottie, however, didn't allow it, feeling a rag at this austere occasion was inappropriate. "How many, many times since then I've wished to my heart that I'd said yes,"[8] she later remarked.

Lottie tried to make it up to her husband by keeping his memory alive. For years she kept their Harlem home open to ragtime composers and musicians who came to discuss, play music, and remember her husband.

Scott Joplin was dead, but the attacks on ragtime continued. A year after Joplin's death, music critic Edward Baxter Perry had this to say in *Étude* magazine:

> Ragtime is syncopation gone mad, and its victims, in my opinion, can only be treated successfully like the dog with rabies, namely, with a dose of lead. Whether it is simply a passing phase of our decadent art culture or an infectious disease which has come to stay, like la grippe and leprosy, time alone can show. . . .[9]

Ironically, by the time this diatribe appeared, ragtime was no longer a threat to the musical establishment. Its dominance as the "bad boy of popular music" had been usurped by a new kind of instrumental music. This music used ragtime's syncopation and dance rhythms but in a looser, freer style and without the overlay of formal European structure. The music was heavily improvisational in nature and its early practitioners, like the first rag musicians, took pop music and adapted it to their own style. As rag players ragged old music in a new way, these musicians "jassed" it up, or gave it rhythm and energy. Hence, its name, first spelled "jass" in an article appearing in the *New York Times* on February 2, 1917, just two months before Scott Joplin's death. A month later, the all-white Original Dixieland Jazz Band made its first recording. Irving Berlin, one of the top composers of Tin Pan Alley, switched his musical allegiance from "Alexander's Ragtime Band" to "Mr. Jazz Himself," his latest song. In 1918, Berlin would reveal the patriotic fervor that would become a hallmark for him, with the awkwardly titled song "Send a Lot of Jazz Bands Over There." "Over There," of course, was the European war front, where American soldiers were then fighting and dying.

While ragtime was losing on the musical front to the newcomer jazz, Scott Joplin's colleagues in ragtime weren't giving up without a fight. Leading the counterattack was John Stark. Despite his falling out with Joplin over finances, the crusty old publisher remained loyal to the classic rag and continued to publish new rags by James Scott, Joseph Lamb, and others into the early 1920s. However, Stark knew he was losing the war and his put-downs of the new music, unlike his earlier attacks on commercial ragtime, had a note of desperation about them. When he was invited to attend a jazz concert conducted by Paul Whiteman, the crowned "King of Jazz," he refused and retaliated by publishing a James Scott rag in 1921 entitled "Don't Jazz Me Rag (I'm Music)."

Through it all, Stark didn't forget the man who had started it all. Shortly after Joplin's death, he published the composer's "Reflection Rag—Syncopated Musings," a composition that bears little resemblance to Joplin's later work. If it is authentic, it may have been written years earlier or was merely an experiment the composer discarded.

When Lottie Joplin had renewed the copyright for "Maple Leaf Rag" in 1916, she had signed it over to Stark, showing she harbored no bitterness toward her husband's longtime publisher. Soon after, Stark retired from the publishing business. He died quietly in St. Louis on November 20, 1926, at the age of eighty-six.

Of the three gifted ragtime composers and colleagues who survived Scott Joplin, perhaps the most praised today is James Scott. His post-Joplin rags include a moving tribute to Joplin's "The Cascades," called "New Era Rag" (1919), and "Troubadour Rag," a rag that used dotted notes to update the rag sound in a valiant attempt to make it more contemporary. The "Modesty Rag" (1920) was more delicate and closer to Joplin's late rags.

Although some rag devotees place Scott's best work above even Joplin's, a more general consensus is that Scott's rags lack the personal, lyrical quality of the older composer's. Terry Waldo calls James Scott "the master craftsman of the form rather than the creative artist."[10] This seems to be borne out by the odd fact that Scott always sent his finished rags to Stark untitled, leaving it up to the inventive publisher to think of an appropriate name. Scott's last rags, while more complex than his earlier ones, show little development and have a narrow emotional range. Like many lesser rag writers, Scott rarely evoked more than one emotion within a single rag. Joplin could evoke two or three.

Scott's last of his thirty-one published rags, "Broadway Rag," appeared in 1922. By then he was living in Kansas City with his wife and working full-time as an organist and musical arranger at the Panama Theater. Some years later he developed chronic dropsy, one symptom of which is swollen fingers. Scott was forced to give up the piano playing he loved so much. He died in a hospital in Springfield, Missouri, on August 30, 1938, his music all but forgotten by the public.

A happier fate lay in store for Joseph Lamb, the only white man in the top ranks of ragtime composers. From 1909 to 1919, Lamb wrote a dozen memorable rags, nearly all of them published by Stark. After "Bohemia Rag" (1919), Lamb decided that if he were to continue to compose he would have to change with the times and so in the early 1920s he began writing what were called "piano novelties." Piano novelties briefly recaptured the classical complexity of ragtime piano music in such pieces as Zez Confrey's best-selling "Kitten on the Keys" (1923). This clever number, which purported to describe the musical journey of a kitten across a keyboard, in its first year actually topped "Maple Leaf Rag" in sheet music sales. One music critic has called piano novelty music "a sort of refined, white suburban extension of ragtime."[11]

But Joseph Lamb's heart was still in classic ragtime and realizing its time had passed, he soon stopped composing altogether. Unlike Joplin and Scott, Lamb had never made a living at music. For him composing rags was a labor of love that was supported by his "day" job in New York's garment district.

In the late 1940s, Rudi Blesh and Harriet Janis, two writers and rag scholars, began working on the first serious book about ragtime, *They All Played Ragtime* (1950). Among the old rag musicians and composers they tracked down and interviewed was Joseph Lamb.

"When we went to see Joe Lamb, he was genuinely surprised that anybody could ever be interested in ragtime anymore," Blesh noted. "When he found out that we weren't kidding him or pulling his leg, he just wanted to open up."[12]

The publicity Lamb received from the book revived interest among rag enthusiasts in his music. Lamb was so inspired by this renewed interest in his work that he actually began writing rags again—in his seventies. In 1959, Folkways Records released an album of Lamb playing his own compositions. It remains one of the very few recordings of a classic rag composer performing his own work. Oddly enough, although the rise of ragtime coincided with the birth of the sound phonograph, piano music did not record well on the earliest phonographs and few, if any, piano rag recordings were made in ragtime's heyday.

Lamb died the following year in Brooklyn, on September 3, 1960. Four years later the Belwin Mills Publishing Corporation published "Ragtime Treasures," which consisted of thirteen new rags by Joseph Lamb. These lovely classic rags showed that Lamb had lost none of his gift for composing over the years. Today many rag experts considered Lamb, who never played in a honky-tonk, to be the "purest" of the classic rag composers. Thanks to the ragtime revival, Lamb kept Scott Joplin's legacy lovingly alive long after ragtime had faded from the musical scene.

Arthur Marshall's brand of rag was quite different from these other artists'. It captured the earthiness and raucous spirit of the saloons in which ragtime was born. In 1916, Marshall's wife died in childbirth and soon after he stopped playing professionally; his last gig was in St. Louis, at Henry Maroche's Moonshine Gardens. The year of Joplin's death, Marshall moved to Kansas City, married his third wife, and retired from the music business. Interviewed and "rediscovered" along with other ragtime greats in later years, Marshall made a home recording of his music in 1956. In 1975, the precious recording was sent to Columbia Records for copying but never arrived; it was accidentally destroyed by the U.S. Postal Service in transit. Fortunately, Marshall never knew this, having died seven years earlier, in 1968, the last of the classic ragtime composers.

Although she wrote no music, Lottie Joplin did what she could to keep her husband's legacy alive. In later years she became friends with Rudi Blesh and showed him unpublished pieces by her husband that no one knew existed, "Pretty Pansy Rag" and "Recitative Rag" among them. She allowed the rag historian to borrow them and let famed black pianist James P. Johnson play them for him. Blesh was struck by their beauty and longed to make copies but promised Lottie he would not. He came to later regret his honesty. According to Blesh, "when Lottie died they [the originals] were turned over to Wilbur Sweatman as executor and they disappeared. And with his death they're gone."[13] One more footnote to the lost legacy of Scott Joplin.

By 1923 "ragtime" as a musical term had lost all meaning. It now referred to any fast, syncopated music usually played on the piano. One of the last classic rags to be published that year was the aptly named "Nitric Acid Rag," by Ed Hudson. Ragtime had all but been disintegrated in the acid bath of hot jazz. Its syncopated beat and infectious rhythms, however, would live on in jazz and just about every other kind of American popular music to come after it, including rhythm and blues and rock and roll.

But in another sense, classic ragtime never really died, it simply fell asleep. The tale of how it was once again awakened is almost as remarkable as its first rise.

THE RETURN OF
SCOTT JOPLIN

I think it's extremely interesting that a thing can be dormant all those years and then can take hold again, and people find it just as fresh and beautiful as it ever was. It makes you wonder about fashion.[1]

—*Rudi Blesh*

As the Roaring Twenties roared on, ragtime, which had once embodied the creative energy and vibrancy of a growing nation, came to express a nostalgia for a simpler, more innocent time. In the postwar era millions of Americans abandoned the country for the booming cities. Technology and industrialism were changing the country as never before.

Ironically, that very technology helped to keep ragtime alive, after a fashion. The silent movies of the 1920s were always accompanied by live music, usually in the form of a piano player. Ragtime was one of the most popular styles in the accompanist's repertoire, especially for those films set in the historical past. When sound films arrived at the decade's end, ragtime continued to be heard on sound tracks and is still heard today in nearly every western that includes a saloon setting. Ragtime had come full circle. It was once again background music.

The only Scott Joplin rag that continued to have a life of its own was his "Maple Leaf Rag." According to David A. Jasen in *Recorded Ragtime*, there were sixty-eight different recordings of it made between 1898 and 1958. The composer himself, however, was all but forgotten. Major works on black musical history of the time, including one written by black composer W. C. Handy, barely mention Joplin's name.

The first stirrings of a ragtime revival took place in the early 1940s. By this time jazz was in something of a creative slump. The early jazz of the 1920s had given way to swing and the big band sound. This music had become increasingly commercialized and watered-down for the widest public consumption. Many jazz bands became increasingly dissatisfied playing this music and turned back to early traditional jazz, which in turn led them to ragtime.

The first of these bands to record rag piano was Lu Watters's Yerba Buena Jazz Band, which in 1941 released recordings of "Maple Leaf Rag" and other classic rags. These recordings attracted new devotees to ragtime and led several specialized jazz magazines to publish articles about ragtime and its leading composer, Scott Joplin. The first of these was "Scott Joplin, Overlooked Genius" by R. J. Carew, which appeared in *The Record Changer* in 1944. Four years later, jazzman Pee Wee Hunt's recording of "Twelfth Street Rag" by white composer Euday Louis Bowman (1887—1949) became a national hit record.

In 1950 the Blesh-Janis book, *They All Played Ragtime*, was published. It fueled the growing interest among musicians and jazz lovers in classic ragtime piano music and helped revive the careers of several ragtime composers, most notably Joseph Lamb. But the popular recording artists of the 1950s who took up ragtime played it in a gimmicky, honky-tonk style that would have been nearly unrecognizable to Scott Joplin and his colleagues. Most of the music came from two pianists, Louis Ferdinand Busch (aka Joe "Fingers" Carr) and Dick Hyman (aka Knuckles O'Toole, Willie "The Rock" Knox, and Slugger Ryan), who put out dozens of best-selling recordings that were fun to listen to but did little to enhance the reputation of ragtime.

Yet there were more serious purveyors of ragtime who tried to place the music in its proper historical context. Among the most prominent of these was entertainer and writer Max Morath, who recalled ragtime's glory days in two popular television series—*The Ragtime Era* and *Turn of the Century*—on educational television in the early 1960s.

In 1961 two ragtime scholars, Trebor Tichenor and Russ Cassidy, founded the *Ragtime Review* , and the following year the Ragtime Society was founded in, of all places, Canada. In 1965, the first annual St. Louis Ragtime Festival was held in the city in which many believe the music was born, and in 1967, a society for the preservation of classic ragtime was formed in Los Angeles, appropriately calling itself the Maple Leaf Club.

But ragtime was still an acquired taste, generally the province of a small but loyal band of followers. It would take the efforts of two young, classically trained musicians to bring the ragtime revival into full bloom.

William Bolcom was a prodigy; he entered the University of Washington at the age of eleven and became the first person to receive a Doctor of Musical Arts degree from Stanford University, in 1964. Two years later, Bolcom, whose tastes in music were decidedly eclectic, accidentally met Rudi Blesh while applying for a Rockefeller grant. Blesh gave Bolcom a copy of Joplin's *Treemonisha* piano score, published by the Ragtime Society.

"I got knocked out by Scott Joplin," Bolcom admitted. "I think he's one of the great guys of all time. He interest-

Max Morath, entertainer and writer, created two
popular educational television series in the early 1960s:
"The Ragtime Era" and "Turn of the Century."

ed me because he was the first American who was able to take all of these various sources of music and synthesize them. . . ."[2]

Bolcom shared his enthusiasm for Joplin with several friends, including composers T. J. Anderson and William Albright. Albright collaborated with Bolcom on several new rags, while Anderson, who was black, was so taken with *Treemonisha* that he began to orchestrate the score with the idea of presenting a full-scale production. Two people Bolcom introduced to Joplin who were to become major figures in the Joplin revival were archivist Vera Brodsky Lawrence and pianist Joshua Rifkin.

Vera Lawrence was a pianist and radio personality who in the 1960s worked on the Ford Foundation Contemporary Music Project. Her job consisted of collecting and cataloging a comprehensive library of the unpublished music of American composers. She had just finished cataloging the complete works of Louis Moreau Gottshalk when Bolcom introduced her to the work of Scott Joplin. It was love at first sight.

"I picked Joplin," Lawrence later wrote, "not because he was black, not because he wrote ragtime, but because he was great."[3] She started collecting the Joplin rags from every source she could find. Such experts and historians as Max Morath gave her many of the rags in sheet music. She placed ads in the magazine *Rag Times* and received responses from collectors and hobbyists.

When she had all the rags, she began looking for a publisher. Her proposal to publish the work of a composer then unknown to the public was not terribly appealing, and twenty-four publishers turned down the project. The New York Public Library, where Lawrence did much of her research, finally stepped in and agreed to publish the work.

The Collected Works of Scott Joplin appeared in two volumes in 1971. Reading a favorable review of the work in the *New York Times*, Max Morath commented that "once Harold Schonberg [music critic for the *Times*] said Joplin was all right, all these classical-music people, who had known about Joplin but disregarded him, decided he was a genius. These are the same people he was up against all his life."[4]

The publication of Joplin's music was a landmark event that was complemented by one of the first serious recordings of Joplin rags. Like Bolcom, Joshua Rifkin, for all his conservatory training, was no musical snob. He loved jazz and first heard "Maple Leaf Rag" when he was ten. "My whole view of ragtime was the conventional one for the time," Rifkin said in an interview. "Ragtime was part of early jazz . . . but when I started looking at it [years later], I discovered that it was something completely different from what I had taken it to be. I began playing the stuff endlessly . . . but just for myself and friends . . . I came to see that it should be played as written, and that's what I did."[5]

Rifkin had recorded several albums of Renaissance music for the small classical label Nonesuch and approached them about doing an album of Joplin rags. The company agreed, feeling it had little to lose. In November 1970, *Piano Rags by Scott Joplin* was released. It consisted of eight rags played in the slow, graceful style Joplin approved of. Nonesuch spent nothing on promoting the album, as was its practice, but slowly, through word of mouth, the album caught on. Within a year, it was a best-seller. Over the next several years Rifkin recorded two more Joplin albums and toured nationally in 1973 and in England the following year. He also played and talked about Joplin's music on public television.

Rifkin's albums were popular with both adults and young people. One of these was the oldest son of Hollywood film director George Roy Hill. "One day in the fall of '72, my oldest son insisted on playing for me [Rifkin's album] about which he was very enthusiastic," Hill later wrote. "Shortly, thereafter, at a family gathering, a thirteen-year-old nephew of mine sat down at the piano and stomped his way through 'Swipesy,' a charming Joplin 'rag,' and between the two of them, they had me hooked. I got the full collection of Joplin 'rags' and started playing through them myself."⁶

At the time, Hill was directing a film called *The Sting*, about two Chicago con artists in the Depression 1930s who give a New York racketeer his comeuppance. "Although Joplin's 'rags' were written before our period, around the turn of the century," Hill noted, "I kept connecting in my mind the marvelous humor and high spirits of his 'rags' with the kind of spirit I wanted to get out of the film."⁷

According to Hill, he tried to score and play the Joplin rags himself for the sound track of his movie, but then, realizing he wasn't a good enough musician, abandoned the idea. He turned for help to Gunther Schuller, another classical musician and conductor, who had recently made his own Joplin album, *The Red Back Book*, based on early orchestrations of Joplin's rags for brass and wind instruments. Other commitments made it impossible for Schuller to score the film, and Hill turned next to an old friend and rising Hollywood film composer, Marvin Hamlisch, who enthusiastically accepted the job.

Hamlisch used Joplin's rags as the basis for nearly the entire score of the film, arranging the music for a small orchestra and piano. Hamlisch claimed the arrangements were his own, but Schuller argued that Hamlisch had lifted them from arrangements on Schuller's own Joplin albums. At the same time, Joshua Rifkin complained that the film's piano solos were taken note for note from his interpretations. Whatever Hamlisch took from these two men, there is no question that the music itself is pure Joplin.

When *The Sting* opened in 1973 it was an immediate hit with audiences and critics alike. The critics praised the performances of Paul Newman and Robert Redford as the con men and Robert Shaw as their quarry. They also lauded the delightful script by David S. Ward and the stylish direction of George Roy Hill. But no less praise was lavished on the memorable score, which reintroduced the extraordinary music of Scott Joplin to the American public. The Joplin rags adapted by Hamlisch for the film included "Gladiolus Rag," Pine Apple Rag," and the sublime "Solace." But the rag that served as The Sting's theme song was "The Entertainer." Unfortunately retitled "The Theme from The Sting," Hamlisch's version of this rag was released as a single record and rose to number 3 on the Billboard charts in April 1974. The movie's sound track album eventually sold more than two million copies.

At the Academy Awards the following March, The Sting won the Oscar for best picture of the year, and Hamlisch received two Oscars, one for best score and another for best song ("The Entertainer"). Scott Joplin's name was barely mentioned. Serious ragtime fans took strong issue with this and were appalled when disc jockeys identified the song on the airwaves as "by Marvin Hamlisch." Their disgust was summed up in a contemporary bumper sticker: "Scott Joplin Got Stung."[8]

Whatever disagreements exist over the music, The Sting put Scott Joplin and ragtime back on the musical map after more than sixty years. Dozens of recording artists turned out ragtime records in the ensuing months, many of them of dubious quality. There were excellent ones, however, and jazz and classical radio stations played the music of Joplin and his contemporaries regularly. Ragtime was no longer seen as nostalgia, novelty, or quaint strains from the past but as integral a part of the American musical landscape as jazz, blues, pop, and rock.

The towns and cities in which Joplin lived, played, and composed got on the bandwagon and paid long-overdue tribute to this great American composer. In 1974, Sedalia, Missouri, held a Joplin festival. Soon after, a memorial plaque honoring Joplin and John Stark was placed at the

*Scene from the motion picture, The Sting,
starring (left to right) Robert Shaw, Robert
Redford, and Paul Newman. The movie score,
comprising adaptations of Scott Joplin's
compositions, reintroduced Joplin's music
to the American public.*

site of the long-gone Maple Leaf Club. Texarkana named a park after its native son. Chicago renamed one of its elementary schools in his honor. St. Louis renovated one of his old homes under the auspices of the Scott Joplin Landmark Preservation Society. And in 1975, representatives of ASCAP (American Society of Composers, Authors, and Publishers) went to St. Michael's Cemetery in Astoria, Queens, and placed a bronze tablet at the gravesite of the composer. It read, simply, Scott Joplin, American Composer 1868–1917.

Also in 1975, Peter Gammond published the first full-length biography of Joplin, *Scott Joplin and the Ragtime Era*. Hollywood gave the composer the star treatment in 1977 with a biographical film starring Billy Dee Williams as Joplin and Art Carney as John Stark.

But perhaps the most significant result of the Joplin revival was the resurrection of his masterpiece, *Treemonisha*. T. J. Anderson's newly orchestrated score for the opera was used in the premiere production of the music department of Morehouse College in Atlanta, Georgia. The all-black cast—under the director Robert Shaw, with choreography by Katherine Dunham—premiered at Atlanta Symphony Hall on January 28, 1972.

The review in *Time* magazine a week later claimed that "Despite its naivete the opera brims with jubilant rhythms and haunting melodies. . . . The gorgeous [choreography of] 'A Real Slow Drag' ended the opera with a ceremonious eroticism that nearly matched Joplin's music."[9]

But not everyone was pleased with the Atlanta production. Vera Lawrence was unhappy with Anderson's orchestrations and persuaded William Bolcom to revise them. The same production, with Bolcom's revisions, was mounted at the Wolf Trap Farm Park in Washington, D.C., in August 1972.

As good as the production was, it was considered only semiprofessional, and Joplin fans eagerly awaited the first fully professional production, by the Houston Opera Company in its spring festival in May 1975. The opera was staged by veteran director Frank Corsaro and orchestrated and conducted by Gunther Schuller. These two gifted artists removed *Treemonisha* from the reality of its Texarkana setting and transformed it into a timeless fantasy fable reinforced by the larger-than-life sets, staging, and costumes. Some critics were enchanted by the transformation, while others preferred the more earthbound Atlanta production, feeling it was closer to the roots of the black experience and Joplin's own conception of the work.

The production was a hit with audiences and later that same year was transported to New York's Broadway, exactly sixty years after the fateful dress rehearsal at Harlem's Lincoln Theatre. At that time, Joplin had told a friend that it would probably take fifty years for his opera to be appreciated. He was off by only ten years.

Vindication came in 1976, during the nation's Bicentennial, when Scott Joplin was posthumously awarded a Pulitzer Prize in music. The award was officially for *Treemonisha*, but in effect it was for a lifework of music unique in his country's history.

TWELVE

AN APPRECIATION

When I first started to research this book, I knew little about ragtime and the man who helped create it. Of course, I had heard the "Maple Leaf Rag" and had seen The Sting, but that was nearly the extent of my knowledge of the music. After listening to a number of Joplin's rags on tape and record, particularly the luminous performances of pianists Joshua Rifkin and James Levine, I have become a convert.

I doubt there exists a casual listener of classic rag. Either the music holds no appeal for you, or you become a devotee. There is no middle ground. Few genres of music have built up as fanatical a following, an enthusiastic army of loyal listeners, fans, and scholars. This seems odd for a brand of music that historically died out about the time of World War I.

Nostalgia for a simpler America may explain part of the appeal of ragtime, but it is the music itself that commands our central attention. In an age in which popular music has taken a bewildering array of forms—from hard rock to country and western—ragtime stands out as unique. There is surely no other American music that has blended together so many different kinds of music—American folk, popular songs, Latin dance, and European forms—into a strikingly original new genre.

But if ragtime is a joy for its listeners, it is doubly so for the musicians skilled enough to master it. "It's so beautifully precise and so symmetrical," Max Morath has said, "yet there's a great, great satisfaction in simply mastering that symmetry just for yourself and feeling the completeness that mastering a rag gives you. There's something extremely mathematical about ragtime. There's a chess-game element."[1]

This "mathematical" element might make you think ragtime can quickly become a mechanical exercise for a musician; nothing could be further from the truth. "I know of no music other than ragtime that I could perform so consistently over so many years and so many times the same pieces . . . and never once fail to enjoy it," says classical conductor and composer Gunther Schuller. ". . . I think it's attributable to this rare combination of a kind of technical perfection of works like those of Joplin and to this other mysterious quality: the inner and genuine and irresistible joy in this music."[2]

Joy is not a word that springs to mind when contemplating the life of the man who made such joyful music. But for all the sorrow, disappointment, and ultimate tragedy of Scott Joplin's life, there must have been great joy and optimism as well. What else could have driven this black man from such humble beginnings to venture into a world of musical composition, a world in which few black Americans had succeeded? What else but joy and supreme determination could have sustained him through the years of playing in sordid honky-tonks, barrooms, and bordellos, resisting the temptations that doomed other just as talented but less determined artists?

But even after he achieved the great success he dreamed of with "Maple Leaf Rag," Scott Joplin was not content. Almost from the beginning of his composing career he yearned to conquer new frontiers, to bring classical and popular music together in ways that had not been attempted before. His very ambitions in this direction, in the end, proved his undoing. One can't but wonder what ending his life and career might have had if he had not written Treemonisha and suffered the anguish of its failure. One looks to the bold experimentation of "Magnetic Rag," his last effort in the genre, and wonders what new synthesis of music Joplin might have created if he had lived as long as some of his contemporaries. Would he have found a way to bring jazz and ragtime together? Would the greatest ragtime composer have become a great jazz composer? It's useless to speculate about what might have been. Joplin's life, like the lives of most human beings, was shaped by the flaws as well as the strengths of his character.

Compromise was not a word he understood. He fought with his closest ally in the music world, John Stark, over the publication of each of his two operas and his ballet. It was this conflict that contributed to their ultimate split. Unwilling to put Treemonisha aside and continue to work on other, more commercial projects, Joplin pushed himself to the limit of endurance, destroying both his health and his financial standing in the process.

But there are positive facets of Joplin's character that are important to remember. Much has been written about John Stark as a businessperson with the soul of an artist, but little has been said about Scott Joplin, the artist with a head for business. Joplin was no Stephen Foster, an impractical artist totally at the mercy of his publishers. Joplin was wise enough to stick with Stark as his publisher, but smart enough to cultivate other publishers as well throughout his career. He was enterprising enough to publish his own work when he found it in his best interest. He formed his own dramatic companies to perform both The Ragtime Dance and A Guest of Honor. If we can rely on the words of his colleagues, such as Arthur Marshall and Sam Patterson, he succeeded in putting together good productions in both cases and even took A Guest of Honor on a successful tour.

Which brings us back to Treemonisha. Here, Joplin the entrepreneur seems to have lost his head completely. Why the obsession with this opera? Without letters, journals, or other personal primary sources, it is difficult to know what was in Joplin's mind during the years he labored on his masterwork. There was the syphilis eating away at his brain and body that certainly must have played a role in his unhealthy fixation.

But, at the same time, it was clear Joplin believed he had reached his creative peak with his grand opera. It is safe to assume that for Joplin, Treemonisha was more than an opera; it was a work that embraced the African-American experience up to that time. It revealed to blacks where they had been in this country and pointed the way to where they should be going. It was both autobiographical and visionary. It came from the deepest level of Joplin's being—as both human being and composer. This can explain the terrible blow he experienced when the opera was flatly rejected by his own people.

Some critics have suggested that if Joplin had conceived of his work as a musical comedy rather than as an opera, Treemonisha might have been a great theatrical success and changed the downward spiral of his life. As intriguing an idea as this is, it seems a mistaken one. Musical comedy in 1915 was still in its infancy. The mature matching of song and libretto was still ten years away with the production of Showboat. Joplin's difficulty would not have been less in writing a libretto for a musical rather than an opera. The opera form, while ill-fitting at times, gives Treemonisha a grandeur and sweep it would not have had as a commercial musical play of the day. The opera's faults are directly related to its author's eccentric and eclectic approach to the form and only add to its strength as an honest and deeply felt work.

But Scott Joplin was more than ragtime's greatest composer and the writer of a uniquely American opera. He also nurtured and supported the entire ragtime movement. He taught, he encouraged and he collaborated with people who would form the nucleus of classic ragtime. Scott Hayden and Louis Chauvin would be forgotten today if not for their extraordinary collaborations with Joplin. He persuaded Stark to publish Joseph Lamb's first rag by lending his support and name to it. He worked with Arthur Marshall on several memorable rags. Joplin's reputation as a generous friend, teacher, and colleague belie his reputation as a distant, aloof figure who cared only about his music.

In both his life and his art, Scott Joplin remained true to his muse. More than fifty years after his death, those efforts have been vindicated. Today he takes his place with the most celebrated of America's composers—Charles Ives, Aaron Copland, Leonard Bernstein. To say nothing of such fellow African-American composers as Duke Ellington, Fats Waller, and Jelly Roll Morton. These musicians owed much to Joplin. He showed them that music could be popular and at the same time enduring. It did not have to be simple to be commercial, it did not have to be crass to be popular, it did not have to be boring to be art.

Like the rags he poured so much love and effort into, Scott Joplin has stood the test of time that is required of all great artists. Today, he is more than the "King of Ragtime," he is a great American composer.

CHRONOLOGY

November 24, 1868 born in Bowie County, Texas,
later part of town of Texarkana
1881–1887 learns to play piano; becomes local musical prodigy; forms instrumental group "The Texas
Medley Quartett"
1888–1892 leaves home to play on the road; works
as itinerant piano player in towns and cities
throughout Midwest, particularly St. Louis
1893 visits and plays at the Chicago World's Fair
1894 leaves fair with new friend Otis Saunders, further
develops rag style of playing in St. Louis and
Sedalia, Missouri
1895 "Please Say You Will" and "A Picture of Her
Face," his first musical compositions, are published
while on the road with the Texas Medley Quartette
1896 three piano pieces, including "The Crush
Collision March," are published
1897 settles in Sedalia
1898 attends George R. Smith College for Negroes;
begins playing at the Maple Leaf Club
1899 publishes his first rag, "Original Rags"; meets
publisher John Stark, who buys and publishes the
"Maple Leaf Rag"

1900   Stark moves publishing operation to St. Louis

1901   Joplin marries Belle Hayden and moves to St. Louis

1902   The Ragtime Dance, a twenty-minute folk ballet, and "The Entertainer" appear

1903   A Guest of Honor, a ragtime opera, is performed, but later lost

1904   writes "The Cascades" in honor of the St. Louis World's Fair; only daughter dies in infancy

1905   separates from Belle; leaves St. Louis and goes back on the road

1906   moves to Chicago briefly, where he composes "Heliotrope Bouquet" with Louis Chauvin

1907   visits family in Texarkana; moves to New York; befriends Joseph Lamb; tours on vaudeville circuit

1908   "The School of Ragtime" is published

1909   marries Lottie Stokes; settles permanently in New York

1910   has final split with John Stark over royalties; "Stoptime Rag" is published

1911   his opera Treemonisha is published

1912   "Scott Joplin's New Rag" appears

1914   "Magnetic Rag," his last rag, is published

1915   Treemonisha is given its first and last performance in Joplin's lifetime at Harlem's Lincoln Theater

1917   enters Manhattan State Hospital on Ward's Island April 1, 1917; dies on Ward's Island

1927   John Stark dies in St. Louis; jazz has replaced rag time as the popular music of America

1941   Lu Watters's Yerba Buena Jazz Band records "Maple Leaf Rag"

1950   They All Played Ragtime by Rudi Blesh and Harriet Janis is published

1967   The Maple Leaf Club, a society for the preserva tion of classic ragtime is founded in Los Angeles

1970   Piano Rags by Scott Joplin performed by Joshua Rifkin is released on Nonesuch Records

1971   The Collected Works of Scott Joplin edited by Vera Lawrence is published

1973 The movie *The Sting*, with a sound track composed of Joplin's music, is released
1975 *Treemonisha* is performed on Broadway
1976 Scott Joplin is posthumously awarded the Pulitzer Prize in music
1983 The U.S. Postal Service issues a commemorative stamp to honor Scott Joplin

THE COMPOSITIONS OF SCOTT JOPLIN

1895 "Please Say You Will"; "A Picture of Her Face" (songs)

1896 "The Crush Collision March"; "Combination March"; "Harmony Club Waltz"

1899 "Original Rags" (arranged by Charles N. Daniels); "Maple Leaf Rag"

1900 "Swipesy Cakewalk" (a rag with Arthur Marshall)

1901 "Peacherine Rag"; "Sunflower Slow Drag" (a rag with Scott Hayden); "The Augustan Club Waltz" (a waltz); "The Easy Winners" (a rag)

1902 "I Am Thinking of My Pickaninny Days" (a song); "Cleopha" (a march); "A Breeze From Alabama" (a rag); "Elite Syncopations" (a rag); "The Entertainer" (a rag); "The Strenuous Life" (a rag); The Ragtime Dance (officially a song, performed as a ballet); "March Majestic" (a march)

1903 A Guest of Honor (ragtime opera); "Something Doing" (a rag with Scott Hayden); "Weeping Willow" (a rag); "Little Black Baby" (a song, words by Louise Armstrong Bristol); "Palm Leaf Rag"

1904 "The Favorite" (a rag); "The Sycamore" (a rag); "The Cascades" (a rag); "The Chrysanthemum" (a rag, subtitled "An Afro-intermezzo"); "Maple Leaf Rag" (a song, lyrics by Sydney Brown)

1905 "Bethena" (a waltz); "Sarah Dear" (a song, words by Henry Jackson); "Bink's Waltz"; Rose-bud (a march); "Leola" (a rag)

1906 "Eugenia" (a rag); "Antoinette" (a march); "The Ragtime Dance" (a rag)

1907 "Searchlight Rag"; "When Your Hair Is Like the Snow" (a song, words by Owen Spendthrift); "Gladiolus Rag"; "Rose Leaf Rag"; "Heliotrope Bouquet" (a rag with Louis Chauvin); "Nonpareil" (a rag)

1908 "Fig Leaf Rag"; "Sugar Cane" (a rag); "Pine-apple Rag";"School of Ragtime—6 Exercises for Piano"

1909 "Wall Street Rag"; "Solace" (a rag, subtitled "A Mexican Serenade"); "Pleasant Moments" (a waltz); "Country Club" (a rag); "Euphonic Sounds" (a rag); "Paragon Rag"

1910 "Stoptime Rag"; "Pine-apple Rag" (a song, words by Joe Snyder)

1911 *Treemonisha* (an opera in three acts); "Felicity Rag" (with Scott Hayden)

1912 "Scott Joplin's New Rag"

1913 "Kismet Rag" (with Scott Hayden); "A Real Slow Drag (from *Treemonisha*); "Prelude to Act 3" (from *Treemonisha*)

1914 "Magnetic Rag"

1915 "Frolic of the Bears" (from *Treemonisha*)

1917 "Reflection Rag"

1971 "Silver Swan Rag" (attributed to Joplin, found on a piano roll)

DISCOGRAPHY

(Most of these recordings, originally issued as records, have also been released as cassette tapes and CDs. All recordings are in stereo.)

Marvin Hamlisch
    "The Sting" (original sound track) MCA-390, reissued as MCA-2040
Dick Hyman
    "Scott Joplin: The Complete Works for Piano" RCA CRL5-1106 (five records, also includes twelve impro-visations on rags and School of Ragtime, with Joplin's text read by Eubie Blake)
James Levine
    "James Levine Plays Scott Joplin" RCA Red Seal ARK1-2243
Max Morath
    "The Entertainer" Arpeggio-1204S
    "The World of Scott Joplin" Vanguard-VSQ30031, SRV3105D
Itzhak Perlman & Andre Previn
    "The Easy Winners and other Rag-Time music of Scott Joplin" Angel-37113 (arranged for violin and piano)

Joshua Rifkin

"Piano Rags by Scott Joplin, Vol. 1" Nonesuch H-71248

"Piano Rags by Scott Joplin, Vol. 2" Nonesuch H-71264

"Piano Rags by Scott Joplin, Vol. 3" Nonesuch H-71305

Gunther Schuller

"Scott Joplin: The Red Back Book" Angel 36060 (conducting the New England Conservatory Ragtime Ensemble)

"Treemonisha" Deutsche Grammophon 2707 (two records, with the Houston Grand Opera)

The Southland Stingers with pianist Ralph Grierson

"Scott Joplin: Palm Leaf Rag and other rags and waltzes" Angel 36074 (arranged for small orchestral ensemble)

"They All Played the Maple Leaf Rag" Archive CD-1600 (twenty-seven versions, including Scott Joplin's piano roll)

SOURCE NOTES

CHAPTER ONE
1. Quoted in Rudi Blesh and Harriet Janis, *They All Played Ragtime* (New York: Oak Publications, 1971).

CHAPTER TWO
1. Katherine Preston, *Scott Joplin: Composer* (New York: Chelsea House, 1988), p. 28.

CHAPTER THREE
1. Ian Whitcomb, *After The Ball: Pop Music from Rag to Rock* (hereafter cited as *After The Ball*) (New York: Penguin, 1972), p. 21.
2. *They All Played Ragtime*, p. 61.
3. Ibid., p. 17.
4. Rudi Blesh, "Scott Joplin," *American Heritage*, June 1975, p. 32.
5. Peter Gammond, *Scott Joplin and the Ragtime Era* (New York: St. Martin's Press, 1976), p. 44.

CHAPTER FOUR
1. Quoted in Gammond, *Scott Joplin and the Ragtime*

Era, pp. 59–60.
2. Quoted in Donald L. Miller, "The White City," *American Heritage,* July-August, 1993, p. 71.
3. Ibid., p. 85.
4. Gammond, *Scott Joplin and the Ragtime Era,* p. 37.
5. Quoted in Blesh and Janis, *They All Played Ragtime,* pp. 42–43.
6. Ibid., p. 44.

CHAPTER FIVE

1. Quoted in Terry Waldo, *This Is Ragtime* (New York: Hawthorne Books, 1976), p. 53.
2. Quoted in Neil Leonard, "The Reactions to Ragtime," in John Edward Hasse, editor, *Ragtime: Its History, Composers, and Music* (hereafter cited as *Ragtime*) (New York: Macmillan, 1985), p. 107.
3. S. Brunson Campbell, "The Ragtime Kid (An Autobiography)" in *Ragtime,* pp. 151–52.
4. Gammond, *Scott Joplin and the Ragtime Era,* p. 123.
5. Ibid., p. 61.
6. Ibid., p. 125.
7. *After The Ball,* p. 19.
8. Quoted in Gammond, *Scott Joplin and the Ragtime Era,* p. 88, *Musical Courier,* 1899.
9. Quoted in ibid., p. 86.
10. Quoted in Leonard, "The Reactions to Ragtime," in *Ragtime,* pp.105–106, *Musical Observer,* September 1914.
11. Leonard, p. 106, *Étude.*

CHAPTER SIX

1. Quoted in Gammond, *Scott Joplin and the Ragtime Era,* p. 66.
2. Ibid., p. 126.
3. Quoted in Blesh and Janis, *They All Played Ragtime,* p. 69.
4. Quoted in Gammond, *Scott Joplin and the Ragtime Era,* p. 66, *St. Louis Globe Democrat.*

5. Blesh and Janis, *They All Played Ragtime*, p. 71.
6. Gammond, *Scott Joplin and the Ragtime Era*, p. 78.
7. David A. Jasen and Trebor Jay Tichenor, *Rags and Ragtime: A Musical History* (hereafter cited as *Rags and Ragtime*) (New York: Seabury Press, 1978), p. 84
8. Blesh and Janis, *They All Played Ragtime*, pp. 79–80.
9. Ibid.

CHAPTER SEVEN

1. "Scott Joplin," *American Heritage*, June 1975, p. 90.
2. Ibid., p. 89.
3. *Rags and Ragtime*, p. 81.
4. Gammond, *Scott Joplin and the Ragtime Era*, p. 72.
5. Ibid.
6. Ibid.
7. *Rags and Ragtime*, p. 108.

CHAPTER EIGHT

1. Quoted in Vera Brodsky Lawrence, "Scott Joplin and Treemonisha," *Treemonisha* libretto accompanying Deutsche Grammophon recording of the Houston Grand Opera production, p. 13.
2. *Treemonisha* libretto, p. 13.
3. Ibid., p. 16.
4. Ibid., p. 21.
5. Ibid.
6. Frank Corsaro, "The Stage Production," *Treemonisha* libretto accompanying Deutsche Grammophon recording of the Houston Grand Opera production, p. 7.
7. *Treemonisha* libretto, p. 22.
8. Gammond, *Scott Joplin and the Ragtime Era*, p. 140.
9. Ibid.
10. Ibid., p. 135.
11. Quoted in Rudi Blesh, "Scott Joplin," *American Heritage*, June 1975, p. 89.
12. Quoted in Gammond, *Scott Joplin and the Ragtime Era*, p. 143.

13. Quoted in Katherine Preston, *Scott Joplin*, p. 94, *American Musician*, June 1911.

CHAPTER NINE
1. Gammond, *Scott Joplin and the Ragtime Era*, pp. 99–100.
2. *This Is Ragtime*, p. 56.
3. Gammond, *Scott Joplin and the Ragtime Era*, p. 148.
4. Quoted in Blesh and Janis, *They All Played Ragtime*, pp. 248–49.
5. Gammond, *Scott Joplin and the Ragtime Era*, pp. 99–100.

CHAPTER TEN
1. Quoted in Edward A. Berlin, *King of Ragtime: Scott Joplin and his Era*, p. 240.
2. Quoted in Preston, *Scott Joplin*, p. 82.
3. Waldo, *This Is Ragtime*, p. 57.
4. Quoted in Gammond, *Scott Joplin and the Ragtime Era*, p. 99, *New York Age*, March 29, 1917.
5. Gammond, *Scott Joplin and the Ragtime Era*, p. 100.
6. Preston, *Scott Joplin*, p. 99.
7. Campbell, "The Ragtime Kid (An Autobiography)" in *Ragtime*, pp.151–152.
8. *They All Played Ragtime*, p. 250
9. Quoted in Waldo, *This Is Ragtime*, p. 48, *Étude*.
10. Ibid., p. 73.
11. Ronald Riddle, "Novelty Piano Music" in Hasse, *Ragtime*, p. 286.
12. Blesh and Janis, *They All Played Ragtime*, p. 185.
13. Ibid.

CHAPTER ELEVEN
1. Blesh and Janis, *They All Played Ragtime*, p. 186.
2. Waldo, *This Is Ragtime*, p. 180.

3. Robert Jones, "Vera Lawrence—an Appreciation" in
   Treemonisha libretto, p. 9.
4. Waldo, *This Is Ragtime*, p. 184.
5. Ibid., p. 181–82.
6. George Roy Hill in program liner notes for the sound
   track album of The Sting, MCA Records, 1973.
7. Ibid.
8. Waldo, *This Is Ragtime*, p. 189.
9. "From Rags to Rags," *Time*, February 7, 1972, p. 89.

CHAPTER TWELVE
1. "Rudi Blesh and the Ragtime Revivalists" in *Ragtime*,
   p. 192.
2. Ibid., p. 196–97.

BIBLIOGRAPHY

BOOKS ABOUT SCOTT JOPLIN

Berlin, Edward A. *King of Ragtime: Scott Joplin and his Era*. New York: Oxford University Press, 1994.

Blesh, Rudi, and Harriet Janis. *They All Played Ragtime*. New York: Oak Publications, 1971.

Evans, Mark. *Scott Joplin and the Ragtime Years*. New York: Dodd, Mead, 1976.

Gammond, Peter. *Scott Joplin and the Ragtime Era*. New York: St. Martin's Press, 1976.

Haskins, James, and Kathleen Benson. *Scott Joplin: The Man Who Made Ragtime*. Garden City, N.Y.: Doubleday, 1978.

Mitchell, Barbara. *Raggin': A Story About Scott Joplin*. Minneapolis: Carolrhoda Books, 1987. Juvenile.

Preston, Katherine. *Scott Joplin*. New York: Chelsea House, 1988. Young adult.

BOOKS ABOUT RAGTIME AND AMERICAN POPULAR MUSIC

Ewen, David. *All The Years of American Popular Music: A Comprehensive History*. Englewood Cliffs, N.J.: Prentice-Hall, 1977.

Haskins, James. *Black Music in America: A History Through Its People*. New York: Thomas Y. Crowell, 1987.

Hasse, John Edward, editor. *Ragtime: Its History, Composers, and Music*. New York: Macmillan, 1985.

Jasen, David A., and Trebor Jay Tichenor. *Rags and Ragtime: A Musical History*. New York: Seabury Press, 1978.

Waldo, Terry. *This Is Ragtime*. New York: Hawthorne Books, 1976.

Wenzel, Lynn, and Carol J. Binkowski. *I Hear America Singing: A Nostalgic Tour of Popular Sheet Music*. New York: Crown, 1989.

Whitcomb, Ian. *After The Ball: Pop Music from Rag to Rock*. New York: Penguin, 1972.

MAGAZINE ARTICLES

Blesh, Rudi. "Scott Joplin." *American Heritage*, June 1975, pp. 27–29, 32, 86–91.

Carson, Gerald. "The Piano in the Parlor." *American Heritage*, December 1965, pp. 54–59, 91.

Miller, Donald L. "The White City." *American Heritage*, July-August 1993, pp. 70–87.

West, Elliot. "Men, Whisky and a Place to Sit." *American History Illustrated*, July 1981, pp. 11–19.

REFERENCE WORKS

Wallechinsky, David, and Irving Wallace. *The People's Almanac*, #3, pp. 621–22. New York: Bantam, 1981.

World Book Encyclopia, (1986 edition), vols. 3, 7, 17, 20.

INDEX

ABOUT THE AUTHOR

Steven Otfinoski has written over fifty books and more than one hundred classroom plays for young adults. The author of biographies of Jesse Jackson, Oprah Winfrey, Nelson Mandela and Boris Yeltsin, he is currently working on a book on rock instrumentals. Mr. Otfinoski is also a playwright and lyricist. His theater company *History Alive!* dramatizes people from American history for students. He lives in Stratford, Connecticut, with his wife, Beverly, an editor and harpist, and their two children.